D1191109

Inflation, Interest, and Growth

Inflation, Interest, and Growth

A Synthesis

Hans Brems
University of Illinois

LexingtonBooks
D.C. Heath and Company
Lexington, Massachusetts
Toronto

Library of Congress Cataloging in Publication Data

Brems, Hans.
  Inflation, interest, and growth.

  Includes index.
  1. Economics—Mathematical models. 2. Economic development—
Mathematical models. 3. Inflation (Finance) and unemployment—Mathe-
matical models. I. Title.
HB141.B718   330'.01'51   78-19226
ISBN 0-669-02466-X

Published simultaneously in Canada

Printed in the United States of America

International Standard Book Number: 0-669-02466-X

Library of Congress Catalog Card Number: 78-19226

To Ulla in gratitude for her patience

Contents

List of Figures

Preface

The purpose of this book is to build models simulating simultaneous unemployment and inflation seen in their natural habitat, that of a growing economy. To simulate growth, models must be dynamic. To simulate anything, models must be solvable—and solved. Confining itself to steady-state growth the book solves for the growth rates of all its variables as well as for the levels of the nominal and real rates of interest. Solutions are examined to see if and how they depend upon the values of the employment fraction and the inflationary potential of the economy.

Early chapters restate separately Wicksellian, Keynesian, monetarist, and neoclassical doctrines to be synthesized in chapter 6—the core of the book. Chapter 6 uses a simple model of a noncorporate closed economy producing a single good from labor, an immortal capital stock of that good, and nothing else. Later chapters add complications like bonds and shares, mortal capital stock, exhaustible and nonexhaustible natural resources, two goods, and two countries.

Primarily this is a book on theory. But references to measurement are frequent and will help the reader decide how good—or bad—its first approximations are.

Over the past four years, chapters or passages of the book were read by colleagues, and most chapters were tried out in workshops and seminars. Particularly helpful were—positive or negative—comments by John S. Flemming, Jørgen Gelting, Ronald Harstad, Donald Hodgman, Wilhelm Krelle, Shlomo Maital, Peter Erling Nielsen, Don Patinkin, Paul A. Samuelson, and Franklin Shupp.

Two research grants by Investors in Business Education in 1977 and 1979 gave me two three-month periods of seclusion needed to begin and complete the final drafting of the book. For clerical and photographic assistance I am grateful to the Department of Economics and the College of Commerce at the University of Illinois.

Acknowledgments

The author is indebted to:

J.C.B. Mohr (Paul Siebeck), Tübingen, for permission to use, in chapter 3, material from H. Brems, "Monetarist and Keynesian Conclusions as Special Cases of a Simple Model of Output and Inflation," *Quantitative Wirtschaftsforschung, Wilhelm Krelle zum 60. Geburtstag,* H. Albach, E. Helmstädter, and R. Henn (eds.), Tübingen 1977, 149–158, now revised and expanded.

The American Economic Association for permission to use, in chapter 4, material from H. Brems, "Reality and Neoclassical Theory," *J. Econ. Lit.,* Mar. 1977, *15,* 72–83, now revised and expanded.

The Cambridge University Press for permission to reproduce as figures 4-6 and 4-7 two illustrations from E.H. Phelps Brown, "Levels and Movements of Industrial Productivity and Real Wages Internationally Compared, 1860-1970," *Econ. J.,* Mar. 1973, *83,* 58–71.

The American Economic Association for permission to use, in chapter 5, material from H. Brems, "Alternative Theories of Pricing, Distribution, Saving, and Investment," *Amer. Econ. Rev.,* Mar. 1979, *69,* 161–165, now expanded.

The Organization for Economic Cooperation and Development, Paris, for permission to reproduce as figure 6-3 an illustration from P. McCracken, G. Carli, H. Giersch, A. Karaosmanoglu, R. Komiya, A. Lindbeck, R. Marjolin, and R. Matthews, *Towards Full Employment and Price Stability, A Report to the OECD by a Group of Independent Experts,* Paris 1977, 314.

Behüt uns, Herr, ... vor Seuchen und vor teurer Zeit.
Deliver us, O Lord, ... from pestilence and times of dearth.

Martin Luther, *"Vater unser im Himmelreich,"* "Our Father which art in Heaven" (1539).

Evangelisches Kirchengesangbuch, Ausgabe für die Evangelisch-lutherschen Landeskirchen Schleswig–Holstein-Lauenburg, Hamburg, Lübeck und Eutin.

Introduction on Method and Scope

Macroeconomics

Current macroeconomics—especially of the monetarist variety—is often impressionistic: models are not fully enough specified to be solvable, hence are not solved. As a result, current macroeconomics is more controversial than current microeconomics. This book is a modest attempt to remove some of the controversy by specification, rigor, and synthesis.

Macroeconomics is the branch of economics interested in the aggregate volume of output rather than its composition and in the price level rather than relative prices. The first nine chapters of the book do their macroeconomics by imagining an economy producing a single good. Here physical output as well as its price are well-defined variables expressible as single numbers.

Statics and Dynamics

A static system determines the level of its variables at a particular time. Technically a static system includes equations in which all variables refer to the same time and in which no derivatives with respect to time occur. Only chapter 2 is static.

This book wants to see unemployment and inflation in their natural habitat, that of a growing economy. Only a dynamic approach can do that. A dynamic system determines the time paths rather than the levels of its variables. Technically it does so by including either difference equations (relating a variable at one time to a variable at a different time) or differential equations (containing derivatives with respect to time). We much prefer differential equations. They are compact and neat. What is more, their operation is greatly facilitated by the use of Euler's number e, the base of the natural logarithms. We use them in chapter 3 and all later chapters.

Steady-State Growth

The dynamic approach adopted in this book is the simplest possible one assuming growth to be steady-state growth. As Hahn and Matthews (1964) did, we define steady-state growth as stationary proportionate rates of growth. Chapter 4 derives five familiar properties of the standard neoclassical growth model, that is, (1) convergence to steady-state growth of output, (2) identical steady-state growth rates of output and capital stock, (3) stationary rate of return to capital, (4) identical steady-state growth rates of the real wage rate and labor productivity, and (5) stationary distributive shares. What is more, chapter 4 finds none of the five properties to be seriously at odds with historical reality. All following chapters confine themselves to steady-state growth.

Unbalanced Growth

As Solow and Samuelson (1953) did, we define balanced growth as identical proportionate rates of growth of physical output for all goods. Real-world growth may be steady-state but is typically unbalanced. Most growth models miss imbalance, for single-good models cannot accommodate it; only multigood models can do so.

In multigood models aggregate physical capital stock and its physical marginal productivity, among other things, cannot be expressed as meaningful and operational single numbers. Post-Keynesians consider this fact somehow very damaging to neoclassical theory. But it is easy to show that physical capital stock and its physical marginal productivity will remain meaningful and operational as matrices, and we show it in chapter 10 considering an economy producing two goods. Chapter 11 considers two countries, each producing its own good.

Solutions

We try to understand economic variables by building models which explain them in terms of something considered the province of other sciences. Technically a model is a system of equations containing variables related to one another through parameters. A parameter is a magnitude fixed by the investigator using information coming from outside the model, such as demographical, geological, psychological, technological, or public-policy information.

Models presented in this book are solvable—and are solved. Almost all solutions are explicit. By an explicit solution for a variable we mean an equation having that variable alone on one side and nothing but parameters on the other side. The book finds such explicit steady-state growth rate solutions for—the price of goods, the nominal rate of interest, the real rate of interest, the money wage rate, the exchange rate, physical consumption, physical investment, physical output, labor employed, physical capital stock, physical marginal productivity of capital stock, the demand for money, the supply of money, and national money income—as well as for the levels of the two rates of interest.

Each chapter of this book begins with a list of symbols carefully distinguishing variables from parameters.

This book avoids the use of the word "constant." As used in the literature, that word sometimes means a parameter, sometimes a variable that happens not to be a function of time, that is, happens to be stationary. Whether or not a variable of ours will be stationary will appear from our growth–rate solutions: stationary variables have zero growth rates.

Reading the Book

The book proceeds gently from the familiar and simple to the less familar and less simple. The first few chapters introduce separately the Wicksellian, Keynesian, monetarist, and neoclassical ideas to be synthesized in chapter 6. Later chapters add complications to the simple model used in chapter 6.

All chapters except 7, 8, and 9 are self–contained and may be read without reading any other chapter. Some repetition will result from such an arrangement but may well be a price worth paying. Each of chapters 7, 8, and 9 has chapter 6 as a prerequisite.

The book uses mathematics all the time but never goes beyond elementary algebra and elementary differential and integral calculus.

References

F.H. Hahn and R.C.O. Matthews, "The Theory of Economic Growth: A Survey," *Econ. J.,* Dec. 1964, *74,* 779-902.

R.H. Solow and P.A. Samuelson, "Balanced Growth under Constant Returns to Scale," *Econometrica,* July 1953, *21,* 412-424.

1 Wicksell: A Dynamic Model of Interest and Inflation

The applications to the bank for money, then, depend on the comparison between the rate of profits that may be made by the employment of it and the rate at which they are willing to lend it.

David Ricardo (1817, ch. 27)

David Hume (1752) described what would happen to prices if "all the money of Great Britain were multiplied fivefold in a night" but failed to describe *how* all that money would find its way into the economy. David Ricardo saw how: banks would be lending money at a rate of interest lower than the rate of profits that could be made by employing it.

Wicksell (1898) restated Ricardo's idea within a rigorously defined framework, three characteristics of which are worth remembering. First— as was inevitable once the rate of profits had been made part and parcel of the money-diffusing mechanism—Wicksell's framework was a lineal descendant of capital theory, specifically the classical "wage-fund" theory. Here, capital advanced wages over a period of production thought of as the harvest year. The money wage rate was found simply by dividing the money wage fund by employment. Second, Wicksell's framework employed such modern concepts as aggregate demand and supply. Third, it was explicitly dynamic—a step-by-step account of how the new money finds its way into the economy. The latter characteristic was lost in the Keynesian revolution.

All references to Wicksell (1898; 1906) use the two English translations, Wicksell (1936; 1935), respectively.

Notation

Variables

$g_P \equiv$ proportionate rate of growth of price

$L \equiv$ labor employed, man–years

$P \equiv$ price of consumers' goods

$r \equiv$ the money rate of interest

$w \equiv$ money wage rate, dollars per man–year

$X \equiv$ physical output of consumers' goods

$Z \equiv$ profits bill

$\zeta \equiv$ the natural rate of interest

Parameters

$F \equiv$ available labor force, man–years

$S \equiv$ available physical capital stock of consumers' goods

Wicksell's Model

The Wage Fund

In his macroeconomics Wicksell (1936: 130) adopted the simple and "prematurely discarded" classical wage–fund doctrine. The period of production is one year "as would be the case if technical conditions firmly prevented any extension or contraction" (1936: 136). Let the economy produce a single consumers' good priced P. Physical capital stock S is a stock of that good, so the money value of capital stock is PS. Let us follow an earlier Wicksell (1893: 94), and let the services of land be free. Then rents will not have to be advanced, only wages will. Consequently in an economy using money the money value of capital stock will equal the wage bill:

$$PS = Lw \qquad (1.1)$$

Temporarily Wicksell wished to visualize an in–kind economy. Here physical capital stock S feeds labor for one year at a real wage rate w/P defined as the number of physical units of consumers' goods a man–year will buy. Wicksell's in–kind vision will emerge when we divide equation 1.1 by P:

$$S = Lw/P \qquad (1.2)$$

Full Employment

Full employment was not an assumption but an equilibrium result:

$$L = F \qquad (1.3)$$

The equilibrating variable was the real wage rate. Paraphrasing the earlier Wicksell (1893: 102), we restate the equilibrating mechanism as follows. If the available physical capital stock could employ more man-years than are available, $L > F$, there is positive excess demand in the labor market, and eager entrepreneurs will bid up the real wage rate until $L = F$. Vice versa, if the available physical capital stock cannot employ all available man-years, $L < F$, there is negative excess demand in the labor market, and eager wage earners will be willing to work at a lower real wage rate until $L = F$. In this way the real wage rate w/P is determined by supply—available labor force F—and demand—available physical capital stock. Remember we are in the nineteenth century!

With the available labor force F fully employed in a one-year period of production, physical output X will be determined.

The Natural Rate of Interest

Such is the in-kind framework within which Wicksell saw his natural rate of interest. Wicksell (1936: 103) failed to define it explicitly, but gave us a hint by describing the profits bill as "the amount by which the total product . . . exceeds the sum of the wages . . . that have to be paid out," or in our notation

$$Z \equiv PX - Lw \qquad (1.4)$$

Divide equation 1.4 by PS, insert equations 1.1 and 1.3, and arrive at an in-kind definition of the natural rate of interest as labor productivity divided by the real wage rate *minus* one:

$$\zeta \equiv Z/(PS) = \frac{X/F}{w/P} - 1 \qquad (1.5)$$

The Money Rate of Interest

Wicksell then introduced money. Between his entrepreneurs and his capitalists he put a bank capable of creating money in the form of drawing rights upon itself. To bridge their one-year gap between input and output, entrepreneurs would borrow from the bank. To hold their assets in an interest-bearing form, capitalists would deposit there. Entrepreneurs would be paying and capitalists earning the same money rate of interest [Wicksell (1936: 140)].

Monetary Equilibrium

Finally Wicksell defined monetary equilibrium as the equality between the money rate and the natural rate of interest:

$$r = \varsigma \tag{1.6}$$

The model now set out works as follows. At the beginning of each year the entrepreneurs borrow the sum $PS = Fw$ from the bank, immediately spend it hiring labor, and embark upon their one–year period of production. Labor's propensity to consume is one. Consequently, receiving the sum Fw, labor immediately spends it on consumer's goods produced the previous year. Those consumer's goods are sold to labor by the capitalists who have an instant part–time job as retailers: at the end of each year they buy that year's output from the entrepreneurs and retain part of it for their own consumption. At the beginning of the following year they sell the rest to labor and deposit the proceeds Fw in the bank.

At the end of each year, according to equation 1.5 the value of output PX will equal $(1 + \varsigma)Fw$. The value of the capitalist-retailers' deposit and the value of the entrepreneurs' debt will both equal $(1 + r)Fw$. Since in monetary equilibrium $r = \varsigma$, the value of output, the assets of the capitalists, and the debt of the entrepreneurs will all be equal. As a result, the capitalist-retailers will be willing and able to buy the output offered by the entrepreneurs at a value enabling the latter to pay their debt to the bank.

Having done so, entrepreneurs are left with no income of their own. This is as it should be. In a purely competitive economy with freedom of entry, anticipated net profits are zero, and in equilibrium realized net profits equal anticipated profits.

Disequilibrium: First Year

Let the bank interrupt such an equilibrium by reducing the money rate by one percentage point. As a result, at the beginning of the first year it looks to the entrepreneurs as if they could make a one percentage point net profit. But anticipated positive net profits are incompatible with pure competition and freedom of entry. The anticipated positive net profits will be washed away by competitive bidding by the entrepreneurs in the labor market raising the money wage rate by approximately 1 percent.

If "approximately 1 percent" is not accurate enough, by exactly how many percent will the money wage rate rise? In equation 1.5 replace ς by r, rearrange, and write

$$(1 + r)w = PX/F \qquad (1.7)$$

At a money wage rate satisfying equation 1.7 entrepreneurs expect a return of no more than the money rate r—a zero net profit. Now on the right-hand side of 1.7 F is a parameter, X is determined by full employment in a one-year period of production, and no change in P is anticipated, because Wicksellian entrepreneurs always expect current prices to prevail in the future. In short, the right-hand side of 1.7 is a constant. Take the derivative of 1.7 with respect to r, rearrange, and find the elasticity

$$\frac{dw}{dr}\frac{r}{w} = -\frac{r}{1+r} \qquad (1.8)$$

For low values of r, $r/(1 + r)$ is not very different from r. For example, if $r = 0.04$, then $r/(1 + r) = 0.0384615$; so if r were reduced by one percentage point from 0.04 to 0.03 or by 25 percent, w would rise by 0.0384615 *times* 25 percent or by 0.9615375 percent, which is approximately 1 percent.

If entrepreneurs are to pay an approximately 1 percent higher money wage rate, they must borrow approximately 1 percent more from the bank, the money supply must expand by approximately 1 percent, and labor will earn and spend approximately 1 percent more. But last year's physical output *minus* the part of it retained by the capitalist-retailers for their own consumption has not changed. Consequently a higher aggregate consumption demand is now chasing an unchanged physical supply, and the price of consumer's goods must rise by approximately 1 percent.

At the end of the first year the entrepreneurs offer that year's physical output to the capitalist-retailers. At the old price and at the new, approximately 1 percent higher, money wage rate satisfying equation 1.7, entrepreneurs expect a return of no more than the money rate r—a zero net profit. At the end of the first year the capitalist-retailers possess a bank deposit no more than adequate to buy the year's physical output at the price anticipated by the entrepreneurs. At the beginning of the year labor spent its approximately 1 percent higher money wage bill, and the capitalist-retailers deposited the proceeds at the money rate of interest r. Consequently on an approximately 1 percent larger deposit the capitalist-retailers have made an exactly one percentage point lower interest rate. Nevertheless, expecting current prices to prevail in the future, the capitalist-retailers are now willing to pay a price approximately 1 percent higher than anticipated by the entrepreneurs. The difference between what they need to do so and what they possess, they borrow from the bank. They will need that difference only for an instant, that is, from the end of the first year to the beginning of the second. Consequently we ignore the interest on it.

Disequilibrium: Second Year

Like the capitalist–retailers, entrepreneurs expect current prices to prevail in the future. Consequently, once again it looks to them as if they could make a one percentage point net profit. But last year the reason was the reduced money rate of interest; this year the reason is the raised price expectation. Whatever the reason, anticipated positive net profits are still incompatible with pure competition and freedom of entry and will be washed away by competitive bidding by the entrepreneurs in the labor market. Once again the money wage rate will rise by approximately 1 percent.

If entrepreneurs are to pay an approximately 1 percent higher money wage rate, they must borrow approximately 1 percent more from the bank, the money supply must expand by approximately 1 percent, and labor will earn and spend approximately 1 percent more. But here at the beginning of the second year, will not the capitalist–retailers retain less for their own consumption? At the beginning of the first year their proceeds were up by an unanticipated approximately 1 percent. If they consider such an increase an instant capital gain rather than income, their income in the first year is indeed down: on an approximately 1 percent larger deposit they made an exactly one percentage point lower interest rate. But this is made up for by the fact that for the first time the entrepreneurs had a realized but unanticipated positive net profit.

As a result of all this, once again a higher aggregate consumption demand is chasing an unchanged physical supply, and once again price must rise by approximately 1 percent.

The Cumulative Process

In this way price will keep rising for as long as the money rate is falling short of the natural rate of interest. Had the money rate been in excess of the natural rate, price would keep falling. Only a restoration of monetary equilibrium could bring such cumulative processes of inflation and deflation to an end.

Figure 1.1 summarizes graphically the simple Wicksellian relationship between the rate of inflation and the money rate of interest.

What Was New in Wicksell, and What Was Missing?

Because Wicksell wanted to deal with inflation, and because inflation is defined as the proportionate rate of growth of price, he needed a dynamic model. He carefully built one by dating his variables and emphasizing the timing of events. This was new.

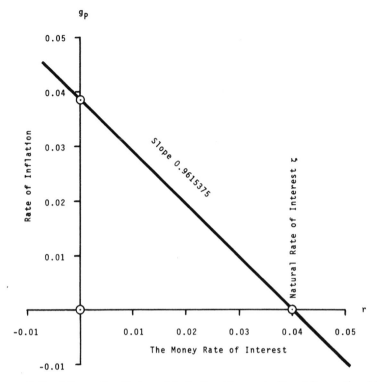

Figure 1-1. Alternative Rates of Inflation Generated by Alternative Money Rates of Interest at a 4 Percent Natural Rate of Interest

Wicksell's distinction between the natural and the money rate of interest enabled him to break the barrier between capital theory and monetary theory and to identify the mechanism through which a quantity theory of money must be operating. A money rate falling short of the natural rate will encourage a demand for money which can be met only by expanding the money supply. Wicksell (1935: 193, 201) emphasized this effect by defining a third rate of interest, the "normal" one, as the rate which could equalize saving and investment, and presumably require no expansion of the money supply.

A money rate falling short of the natural rate will generate inflation. Wicksell (1936: 102) emphasized this effect be defining a fourth rate of interest, the "neutral" one, as the rate which would keep prices stationary. All this was also new.

Is a normal rate of interest also a neutral one? Wicksell thought so. But under late–twentieth–century assumptions an interest rate at which saving equals investment will not guarantee absence of inflation , as we shall see in chapter 6. More generally, late-twentieth-century readers will find at least four ideas missing in Wicksell. First, physical output as a variable; second, liquidity preference; third, Fisher's distinction between a nominal rate of interest and a real one; and fourth, cost-push inflation. Let us look very briefly at these four ideas.

Physical Output as a Variable

To Wicksell was physical output ever a variable? Arguing against the Tooke-Fullarton banking principle, Wicksell (1935: 195) was prepared to modify his argument "if previously there had been unemployment" but continued:" But all these are secondary considerations. As a first approximation we are entitled to assume that all production forces are already fully employed."

To the Wicksellian Ohlin (1933; 1934) physical output was a variable, as it was to be to Keynes (1936) two years later. But Ohlin's feedback between physical output and aggregate demand was not telescoped into an instant static equilibrium along a physical–output axis, as the Keynesian one was to be. Ohlin's feedback unfolds in a cumulative process along a time axis, as did the Wicksellian one between prices and aggregate demand.

Liquidity Preference

Nobody in the Wicksellian model holds money in liquid form. Money comes into existence as a loan to entrepreneurs who immediately spend it hiring labor. Labor immediately spends it buying consumers' goods. Capitalist-retailers hold their assets in interest–bearing form.

The Wicksellian Ohlin (1934: 42, 69, 85) saw liquidity preference and— like Keynes two years later—explained it in terms of speculation in bond prices. Asset holders will hold bonds rather than money when the bond yield is high. They will hold money rather than bonds when the bond yield is low.

Fisher's Nominal and Real Rates of Interest

Neither Wicksell nor Keynes accepted Fisher's (1896) distinction between a nominal rate (the rate of interest in terms of gold) and a real rate (the rate of interest in terms of wheat or other goods). Wicksell (1936: 165–166) knew Fisher's work, then only two years old, and restated its "logical basis" by saying that "entrepreneurs incur their 'expense' (wages, rents, etc.) when things are cheap, and dispose of their product after prices have gone up." Strangely enough Wicksell was unimpressed: "Such a rise in prices . . . does not provide [the entrepreneurs] with the means of paying a higher rate of interest." Wicksell must have identified himself with his entrepreneurs who would never anticipate such a rise in prices, because they always expect current prices to prevail in the future.

Cost-Push Inflation

Wicksellian inflation was always of the pure demand-pull variety. Theorists had to wait for another sixty years for cost-push inflation in the form of the Phillips (1958) curve: within their province but tempered by unemployment, labor unions will seek a relative gain by raising the money wage rate. Theorists had to wait even longer before labor's inflationary expectations were incorporated into the Phillips curve: instead of always expecting current prices to prevail in the future, labor learns from experience. By expecting inflation labor is compelled to contribute to it.

In the following chapters we shall examine such missing ideas and attempt a synthesis of them.

References

I. Fisher, "Appreciation and Interest," *Publications of the American Economic Association*, Aug. 1896, *11*, 331–442.

D. Hume, "Of Money," *Political Discourses*, Edinburgh 1752.

J.M. Keynes, *The General Theory of Employment, Interest, and Money*, London 1936.

B. Ohlin, "Till frågan om penningteoriens uppläggning," *Ekonomisk Tidskrift 35*, 1933, 45–81. "On the formulation of Monetary Theory," *Hist. Polit. Econ.*, Fall 1978, *10*, 353–388.

———, *Penningpolitik, offentliga arbeten, subventioner och tullar som medel mot arbetslöshet*, Stockholm 1934, summarized in *Hist. Polit. Econ.*, Fall 1978, *10*, 400–412.

A.W. Phillips, "The Relation between Unemployment and the Rate of Change of Money Wage Rates in the United Kingdom, 1861–1957," *Economica*, Nov. 1958, *25*, 283–299.

D. Ricardo, *Principles of Political Economi and Taxation*, London 1817.

K. Wicksell, *Ueber Wert, Kapital und Rente*, Jena 1893 and London 1933.

———, *Geldzins und Güterpreise*, Jena 1898. *Interest and Prices*, London 1936.

———, *Föreläsningar i nationalekonomi, II*, Lund 1906. *Lectures on Political Economy, II*, London 1935.

2 Keynes: A Static Model of Interest and Output

*But there is one word in the book that cannot be defended . . . the word
"general."*   J.A. Schumpeter (1951:286)

In Keynes's static equilibrium, interest and physical output were the equilibrating variables. Using four simplifications let us set out the essence of such an equilibrium.

First, let prices be frozen. Keynes (1936, ch. 21, p. 296) did observe that "instead of constant prices in conditions of unemployment, and of prices rising in proportion to the quantity of money in conditions of full employment, we have in fact a condition of prices rising gradually as employment increases." But the chapter came after the party was over: chapter 21 is the last of the main body of the book.

Second, let us consider only one rate of interest. At frozen prices there will be no need for a distinction between a nominal and a real rate of interest, and Keynes never applied such a distinction.

Third, let us consider only one good. In *General Theory,* Keynes paid no attention to relative prices and their role in encouraging substitution among goods in consumption or production. To all intents and purposes his model was a model of one good serving interchangeably as a consumers' or a producers' good.

Fourth, let us write a linear model. To be sure Keynes (1936, ch. 15) did discuss the "possibility" of an infinite interest elasticity of his liquidity–preference function. But the idea of such a liquidity trap has later been discredited by empirical research from Bronfenbrenner and Mayer (1960) to Barth, Kraft, and Kraft (1976).

Notation

Variables

C ≡ physical consumption
D ≡ demand for money
I ≡ physical investment
r ≡ rate of interest
X ≡ physical output

Parameters

A ≡ autonomous consumption
a ≡ marginal propensity to consume
B ≡ autonomous investment
b ≡ marginal inducement to invest
f ≡ marginal inducement to hold money as an asset
J ≡ autonomous demand for money
j ≡ marginal propensity to hold transaction money
M ≡ supply of money
P ≡ price of good

The model will include no derivatives with respect to time, hence is static. Let all parameters be positive.

A Keynesian Model

We begin with the goods market and write consumption demand as a function of output:

$$C = A + aX \qquad (2.1)$$

shown in figure 2-1. Using nonhomogeneous[a] functions we must make up our minds whether we want them to hold in money or real terms. Our consumption function 2.1 holds in real terms: multiply it by price P, find $CP = AP + aPX$, and see that at a given X, doubling P would double CP but leave C unaffected. There is no money illusion! (A consumption function holding in money terms would have been of the form $CP = A + aPX$; here doubling P would have affected C.)

Let investment demand be a function of the rate of interest:

$$I = B - br \qquad (2.2)$$

shown in figure 2-2. Our investment function 2.2 holds in real terms, too: multiply it by price P, find $IP = BP - bPr$, and see that at a given r, doubling P would double IP but leave I unaffected. There is no money illusion!

Finally let goods market equilibrium require the supply of goods to equal the demand for them:

$$X = C + I \qquad (2.3)$$

---

[a] Homogeneous functions (to be used in chapter 4 and all later chapters) have no constant term, consequently hold in money as well as real terms. No need to make up one's mind!

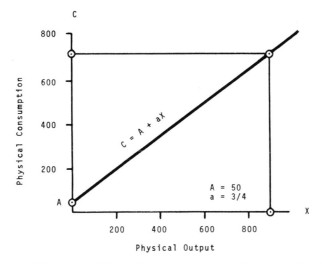

Figure 2-1. A Keynesian Linear Nonhomogeneous Consumption Function

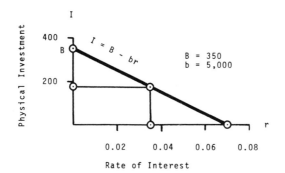

Figure 2-2. A Keynesian Linear Nonhomogeneous Investment Function

So much for the goods market. Now for the money market. Let the real demand for money be a function of output and the rate of interest:

$$D/P = J + jX - fr \qquad (2.4)$$

shown in figure 2-3. Our demand-for-money function 2.4 holds in real terms, too: multiply it by price P, find $D = JP + jPX - fPr$, and see that at a given r and a given X doubling P would double D but leave D/P unaffected. Again there is no money illusion.

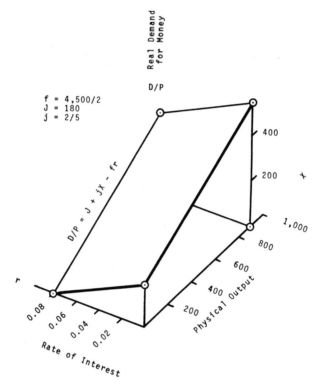

Figure 2-3. A Keynesian Linear Nonhomogeneous Money Demand
Function

Money-market equilibrium requires the supply of money to equal the
demand for it:

$$M = D \qquad (2.5)$$

where the money supply M is a parameter to be manipulated at will.

Equilibrium Solutions

Algebraic Solutions

Keynes solved for the rate of interest and the level of output:

$$r = \frac{(A + B)j - (1 - a)(M/P - J)}{(1 - a)f + bj} \qquad (2.6)$$

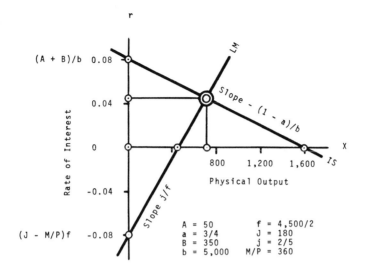

Figure 2-4. Hicksian *IS* and *LM* Curves Drawn in the Same Diagram

$$X = \frac{(A + B)f + b(M/P - J)}{(1 - a)f + bj} \tag{2.7}$$

Graphical Solution

Textbooks often solve graphically by applying Hicksian *IS* and *LM* curves. Does our model have such curves? Take equations 2.1–2.3 together and find the equation of our *IS* curve, $r = [A + B - (1 - a)X]/b$, shown in figure 2-4. Take 2.4 and 2.5 together and find the equation of our *LM* curve, $r = (J - M/P + jX)/f$, also shown in figure 2-4. The solutions for r and X are simply the ordinate and the abscissa, respectively, of the intersection point between the *IS* and the *LM* curve.

Effects of Monetary Policy

Effect upon the Rate of Interest

To find how sensitive our solution 2.6 for the rate of interest is to monetary policy, differentiate it with respect to M/P:

$$\frac{\partial r}{\partial (M/P)} = -\frac{1 - a}{(1 - a)f + bj} \tag{2.8}$$

As long as the propensity to save $1 - a$ is positive, our derivative 2.8 is negative: expanding the money supply will lower the interest rate. In figure 2-4 such an expansion would appear as a downward shift of the the LM curve—its intercept with the r-axis, $(J - M/P)/f$, is now lower. Consequently the ordinate of the intersection point between the IS and LM curves will be lower.

Effect upon Output

To find how sensitive our solution 2.7 for output is to monetary policy, differentiate it with respect to M/P:

$$\frac{\partial X}{\partial (M/P)} = \frac{b}{(1 - a)f + bj} \qquad (2.9)$$

All parameters were assumed to be positive, consequently our derivative 2.9 is positive: expanding the money supply will raise output. In figure 2-4 such an expansion would appear as a downward shift of the LM curve, hence raise the abscissa of the intersection point between the IS and LM curves.

We can no longer ignore inflation. Can our model be modified to accommodate inflation, and with it the two rates of interest? In chapter 3 let us try.

References

J. Barth, A. Kraft, and J. Kraft, "Estimation of the Liquidity Trap Using Spline Functions," *Rev. Econ. Statist.,* May 1976, *58,* 218–222.

M. Bronfenbrenner and T. Mayer, "Liquidity Functions in the American Economy," *Econometrica,* Oct. 1960, *28,* 810–834.

J.M. Keynes, *The General Theory of Employment, Interest, and Money,* London 1936.

J.A. Schumpeter, *Ten Great Economists from Marx to Keynes,* New York 1951.

3 Could Keynes and Monetarists Coexist in a Semidynamic Model of Inflation?

... la cause même qui augmente la quantité de l'argent au marché et qui augmente le prix des autres denrées ... soit précisément celle qui augmente le loyer de l'argent ou le taux de l'intérêt.

Anne Robert Jacques Turgot (1769–70).

... a being ... the rate of appreciation of gold in terms of wheat. Let the rate of interest in gold be i, and in wheat be j. Our result ... is 1 + j = (1 + a) (1 + i).

Irving Fisher (1896: 8–9).

Keynes's strength was his variable physical output. His weakness was his frozen price.

To build an inflation model we must first unfreeze price. But it would not do merely to take price P out of our list of parameters and put it into our list of variables, and to add another equation to our static system, say an aggregate supply curve. No static model can determine anything else than the levels of its variables, and the resulting system would merely tell us how high the equilibrium level of price P would be.

It is one thing to tell how high price would be. It is quite a different thing to tell how rapidly price is changing—which is what inflation is all about. Only a dynamic model can do that.

Once we have a dynamic model telling us how rapidly price is changing, we must have not one rate of interest but two. Keynes, who paid less attention to price as a variable, did not appreciate Fisher's distinction between a nominal rate (the rate of interest in terms of gold) and a real rate (the rate of interest in terms of wheat or other goods).[a] That distinction is the strength of monetarists from Turgot (1769–1770) to Mundell (1971). The weakness of monetarists is the scant attention they pay to physical output.

Let us borrow the best from Keynes and the monetarists and try to avoid their weaknesses.

---

[a] Keynes (1936: 222–229) did consider "own rates" of interest like a wheat rate of interest, a copper rate of interest, and so on, and discussed their carrying-cost and liquidity aspects. On pp. 142–143 he discussed Fisher's (1896) aspect of such own rates but remained unconvinced.

Notation

Variables

C ≡ physical consumption
D ≡ demand for money
g_P ≡ rate of inflation
I ≡ physical investment
P ≡ price of good
r ≡ nominal rate of interest
ϱ ≡ real rate of interest
X ≡ physical output

Parameters

A ≡ autonomous consumption
a ≡ marginal propensity to consume
B ≡ autonomous investment
b ≡ marginal inducement to invest
f ≡ marginal inducement to hold money as an asset
H ≡ rate of inflation at zero excess capacity
h ≡ sensitivity of rate of inflation to excess capacity
J ≡ autonomous demand for money
j ≡ marginal propensity to hold transaction money
M ≡ supply of money
X_{max} ≡ physical capacity

  The model will include one derivative with respect to time t, hence is dynamic. Let all parameters be positive.

A Keynesian–Monetarist Model

If our model is to deal with inflation, it can no longer be static. We introduce our dynamics sparingly and begin with an absolute minimum of it. Define the proportionate rate of growth of price as

$$g_P \equiv \frac{dP}{dt}\frac{1}{P} \tag{3.1}$$

and define the real rate of interest as the nominal one *minus* that proportionate rate of growth:

$$\varrho \equiv r - g_P \tag{3.2}$$

Within their province but tempered by excess capacity, firms will seek a relative gain by raising price P:

$$g_P = H - h(X_{\max} - X) \qquad (3.3)$$

as shown in figure 3-1. As before, let consumption demand be a function of output:

$$C = A + aX \qquad (3.4)$$

as shown in figure 3-2. Let investment demand be a function of the real rate of interest:

$$I = B - b\varrho \qquad (3.5)$$

as shown in figure 3-3. Why should investment demand be a function of the real rather than the nominal rate of interest? Physical investment is the acquisition of the physical good itself. The price of that good is growing at the rate g_P, hence the return on it tends to be the sum of a real rate of interest ϱ and a capital gain g_P. Consequently investment would not be discouraged by a nominal rate of interest that was high merely because of inflation; only "an increase in the real interest rate lowers investment," Mundell (1971: 16).

Goods–market equilibrium requires the supply of goods to equal the demand for them:

$$X = C + I \qquad (3.6)$$

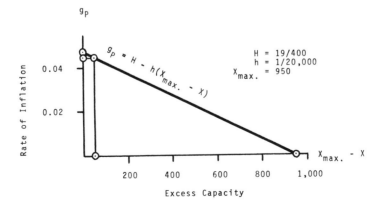

Figure 3-1. Inflation Tempered by Excess Capacity

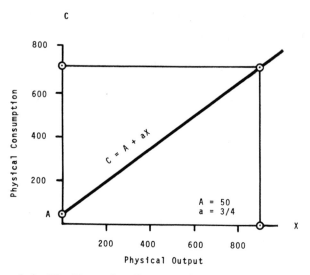

Figure 3-2. The Keynesian Consumption Function Once Again.

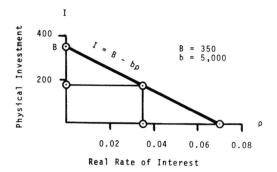

Figure 3-3. Investment as a Function of the Real Rate of Interest

So much for the goods market. Let the real demand for money be a function of output and the nominal rate of interest:

$$D/P = J + jX - fr \qquad (3.7)$$

as shown in figure 3-4. Why should the demand for money be a function of the nominal rather than the real rate of interest?

Keynes himself made no distinction between the two rates, and only his nontransaction demand for money was a function of the rate of interest in

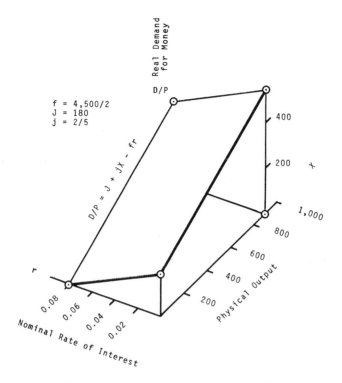

Figure 3-4. Real Demand for Money as a Function of Physical Output and the Nominal Rate of Interest

the first place. When the bond yield was high, asset holders would hold bonds rather than money because they expected bond prices to rise. When the bond yield was low, asset holders would hold money rather than bonds because they expected bond prices to fall. So it was the bond yield that mattered, and the bond yield is a nominal rather than a real rate of interest.

Baumol (1952) and Tobin (1956) emphasized the opportunity cost of holding money for transaction purposes. Rather than holding money in the form of noninterest–bearing demand deposits one may hold interest–bearing savings deposits. Here the foregone opportunity is the nominal rate of interest on the latter. Indeed there is a whole range of foregone opportunities: rather than holding money one may hold equity in the physical good or hold that good itself. The price of the good is growing at the rate g_P, hence the foregone opportunity is the sum of a real rate of interest ϱ and a capital gain g_P. According to equation 3.2 that sum will be the nominal rather than the real rate of interest.

Money-market equilibrium requires the supply of money to equal the demand for it:

$$M = D \qquad (3.8)$$

where the money supply M is a parameter to be manipulated at will.

Equilibrium Solutions

Algebraic Solutions

Keynesian-monetarist issues have to do with four variables, that is, the rate of inflation, the two rates of interest, and output. For those four variables we find the following algebraic solutions:

$$g_P = \frac{(A + B)fh + [(1 - a)f + bj](H - hX_{max}) + bh(M/P - J)}{(1 - a - bh)f + bj} \qquad (3.9)$$

$$r = \frac{[A + B + b(H - hX_{max})]j - (1 - a - bh)(M/P - J)}{(1 - a - bh)f + bj} \qquad (3.10)$$

$$\varrho = \frac{(A + B)(j - fh) - (1 - a)[f(H - hX_{max}) + M/P - J]}{(1 - a - bh)f + bj} \qquad (3.11)$$

$$X = \frac{(A + B)f + b[f(H - hX_{max}) + M/P - J]}{(1 - a - bh)f + bj} \qquad (3.12)$$

A Graphical Solution

Would the Hicksian $IS - LM$ curve technique work once again? Not as easily as before. Take equations 3.4–3.6 together and find the equation of our IS curve: $\varrho = [A + B - (1 - a)X]/b$, shown in the upper half of figure 3–5. Take 3.7 and 3.8 together and find the equation of our LM curve: $r = (J - M/P + jX)/f$, shown in the lower half of figure 3–5. Now could we let our IS and LM curves intersect each other? We cannot, for they are drawn in different systems of coordinates. In the upper half of figure 3–5 the vertical axis is ϱ; in the lower half it is r. According to definition 3.2 the difference between r and ϱ is the rate of inflation g_P. That difference would be zero only in the absence of inflation. Before we can let our IS and LM curves intersect each other, we must draw them in the same system of coordinates; for example by inserting our hitherto unused equations 3.2 and 3.3

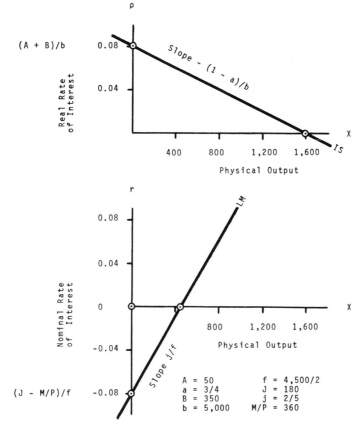

Figure 3–5. Hicksian *IS* and *LM* Curves Now Belong in Separate Systems
of Coordinates

into the equation of our *IS* curve and write the latter: $r = [A + B + b(H - hX_{max}) - (1 - a - bh)X]/b,$ shown in figure 3–6. Compared with the *IS* curve of figure 3–5 the new *IS* curve has both a new slope and a new intercept with the vertical axis. What is new is the appearance of the price–policy parameters H and h and the capacity X_{max}. Now our *IS* and *LM* curves may be drawn in the same system of coordinates and will intersect each other, as shown in figure 3–6.

Numerical Illustration

Our model is one of a purely private closed economy. It is too simple to permit econometric estimates of its parameters, so the following numerical

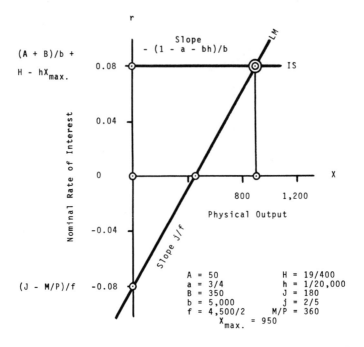

Figure 3-6. Using Price–Policy Parameters H and h as well as Capacity X_{max} to Bring IS and LM Curves Together in the Same System of Coordinates

illustration will have to do. Consider the U.S. economy around 1972 but purge it of net export and government purchases. A stylized description of what remains would be:

$$
\begin{aligned}
C &= 725 \text{ billion dollars per annum} \\
g_P &= 0.045 \text{ per annum} \\
I &= 175 \text{ billion dollars per annum} \\
D/P &= 360 \text{ billion dollars} \\
r &= 0.08 \text{ per annum} \\
\varrho &= 0.035 \text{ per annum} \\
X &= 900 \text{ billion dollars per annum}
\end{aligned}
$$

Postulate the parameters of the consumption function as well as the following elasticities around the 1972 point. Let the real–interest elasticity of investment be − 1; let the elasticity of the rate of inflation with respect to output (not excess capacity) be + 1; and let the output elasticity of the real demand for money be + 1. Finally rely on Boorman's (1976: 315–360) survey of empirical work on the nominal–interest elasticity of the real demand for money and let it be − ½. Then our parameters would be:

$$
\begin{array}{ll}
A = 50 & H = 19/400 \\
a = 3/4 & h = 1/20,000 \\
B = 350 & J = 180 \\
b = 5,000 & j = 2/5 \\
f = 4,500/2 & M/P = 360 \\
& X_{\max} = 950
\end{array}
$$

Inserting these parameter values into our behavior equations will give us the curves shown in figure 3-1 through 3-4. Inserting them into our solutions 3.9 through 3.12 will give us the values 0.045, 0.08, 0.035, and 900 for g_P, r, ϱ, and X, respectively, that is, the stylized 1972 values. Now let us find impact multipliers.

Effects of Monetary Policy

The Effect upon the Rate of Inflation

To find how sensitive our solution 3.9 for the rate of inflation is to monetary policy, differentiate it with respect to M/P:

$$
\frac{\partial g_P}{\partial (M/P)} = \frac{bh}{(1 - a - bh)f + bj} = 1/8,000 \tag{3.13}
$$

using our numerical illustration. The derivative 3.13 has the dimension pure number per annum per unit of real money supply and is invariant with M/P. By contrast, the elasticity

$$
\frac{\partial g_P}{\partial (M/P)} \frac{M/P}{g_P} = 1
$$

would be dimensionless but would vary with M/P. Its value 1 holds only in the immediate neighborhood of the 1972 point. The derivative 3.13 is positive: the monetarists are right that expanding the real money supply will accelerate inflation.

The Effect upon the Nominal Rate of Interest

To find how sensitive our solution 3.10 for the nominal rate of interest is to monetary policy, differentiate it with respect to M/P:

$$
\frac{\partial r}{\partial (M/P)} = -\frac{1 - a - bh}{(1 - a - bh)f + bj} = 0 \tag{3.14}
$$

using our numerical illustration. The derivative 3.14 has the dimension pure number per annum per unit of real money supply and is invariant with M/P. By contrast, the elasticity

$$\frac{\partial r}{\partial(M/P)} \frac{M/P}{r} = 0$$

would be dimensionless but would vary with M/P. In our numerical illustration the effect upon the nominal rate of interest happens to be zero. But had the marginal propensity to consume been lower, the marginal inducement to invest been lower, or the rate of inflation been less sensitive to excess capacity, then expanding the real money supply would have lowered the nominal rate of interest.

Conversely, had the marginal propensity to consume been higher, the marginal inducement to invest been higher, or the rate of inflation been more sensitive to excess capacity, expanding the real money supply would have raised the nominal rate of interest.

The Effect upon the Real Rate of Interest

To find how sensitive our solution 3.11 for the real rate of interest is to monetary policy, differentiate it with respect to M/P:

$$\frac{\partial \varrho}{\partial(M/P)} = - \frac{1 - a}{(1 - a - bh)f + bj} = -1/8{,}000 \qquad (3.15)$$

using our numerical illustration. Again the derivative has the dimension pure number per annum per unit of real money supply and is invariant with M/P. The elasticity

$$\frac{\partial \varrho}{\partial(M/P)} \frac{M/P}{\varrho} = -9/7$$

would be dimensionless but would vary with M/P. We are pleased to notice that the sum of our derivatives 3.13 and 3.15 equals our derivative 3.14, as it should according to equation 3.2. Our derivative 3.15 is negative: expanding the real money supply will lower the real rate of interest.

The Effect upon Output

To find how sensitive our solution 3.12 for output is to monetary policy, differentiate it with respect to M/P:

$$\frac{\partial X}{\partial (M/P)} = \frac{b}{(1 - a - bh)f + bj} = 5/2 \tag{3.16}$$

using our numerical illustration. Since output is measured in goods per annum, and real money supply is measured in goods, the dimension of equation 3.16 is a pure number per annum. The derivative 3.16 is invariant with M/P. The elasticity

$$\frac{\partial X}{\partial (M/P)} \frac{M/P}{X} = 1$$

would be dimensionless but would vary with M/P. The derivative 3.16 is positive: an expanding real money supply does raise output.

Conclusions

Keynesians and Monetarists

To some extent disagreements between Keynesians and monetarists are on parameter values. Our derivatives 3.13 and 3.14, for example, are particularly controversial, and their values depend very much on the parameter values adopted for the marginal propensity to consume a, the marginal inducement to invest b, and the sensitivity of the rate of inflation to excess capacity h. Consider Keynesians and monetarists in turn.

A very Keynesian proposition was that the marginal propensity to consume was less than one. Keynes himself was primarily concerned with a depressed economy. Here, amidst uncertainty and pessimism, the rate of interest would make little difference in investment decisions, so the marginal inducement to invest b would be small. When the Phillips (1958) curve made its appearance, some Keynesians accepted its trade-off between inflation and unemployment, but others had a reservation. The trade-off may be ineffective because the sensitivity of inflation to excess capacity h may be low. Now if both b and h are small, so is their product bh and with it our derivative 3.13: Keynesians de-emphasize the effect of the real money supply upon the rate of inflation. And if the product bh is small, then perhaps $1 - a - bh > 0$, and our derivative 3.14 may be negative: Keynesians expect an expanding real money supply to lower the nominal rate of interest.

The permanent income hypothesis of the monetarists makes consumption even less sensitive to current income than Keynes did. No disagreement here: $a < 1$. Monetarists tend to believe in the price mechanism including an investment–interest relationship: the marginal inducement b may be substantial. Like some Keynesians, monetarists have a reservation about the Phillips curve—but the opposite one: the trade-off is ineffective because the sensitivity of inflation to excess capacity h is high! Now if both b and h are large, so is their product bh and with it our derivative 3.13. Monetarists emphasize the effect of the real money supply upon the rate of inflation. And if the product bh is large, then perhaps $1 - a - bh < 0$, and our derivative 3.14 may be positive: monetarists expect an expanding real money supply to raise the nominal rate of interest rather than lowering it.

In our own numerical illustration $1 - a - bh$ happens to be exactly zero. The slightest revision, then, of our crude parameter values might validate either Keynesian or monetarist views.

Statics, Semidynamics, and Full Dynamics

Notice the contrast to chapter 2: there the Keynesian model was resting in its static equilibrium. The present model is never fully at rest. Parts of it are moving, other parts are not. Notice the similarity to chapter 1: much the same parts were moving and not moving, respectively, in the Wicksellian model. According to solutions 3.9 through 3.12, our rate of inflation g_P, our rates of interest r and ϱ, and our physical output X will remain at rest as long as the real money supply M/P does. The nominal money supply M nowhere occurs alone; it is everywhere divided by price P. Consequently, for the ratio M/P to remain at rest, the nominal money supply must be growing at the same rate as does price P.

Our semidynamic model of inflation is only a beginning, and we have work to do. All parts of our model should be moving: every variable deserves to be seen in its natural habitat, a growing economy. We cannot see all of them there at once. Chapter 4 will merely provide the necessary fully dynamic setting. Temporarily, in chapters 4 and 5, unemployment and inflation will disappear from view. But they will reappear in chapter 6.

References

W.J. Baumol, "The Transactions Demand for Cash: An Inventory Theoretic Approach," *Quart. J. Econ.,* Nov. 1952, *66,* 545–556.

J.T. Boorman, "The Evidence on the Demand for Money: Theoretical Formulations and Empirical Results," in T.M. Havrilesky and J.T. Boorman (eds.), *Current Issues in Monetary Theory and Policy,* Arlington Heights, Ill., 1976, 315–360.

I. Fisher, "Appreciation and Interest," *Publications of the American Economic Association,* Aug. 1896, *11,* 331–442.

J.M. Keynes, *The General Theory of Employment, Interest, and Money,* London 1936.

R.A. Mundell, *Monetary Theory: Inflation, Interest, and Growth in the World Economy,* Pacific Palisades 1971.

A.W. Phillips, "The Relation between Unemployment and the Rate of Change of Money Wage Rates in the United Kingdom, 1861-1957," *Economica,* Nov. 1958, *25,* 283-299.

J. Tobin, "The Interest-Elasticity of Transactions Demand for Cash," *Rev. Econ. Statist.,* Aug. 1956, *38,* 241-247.

A.R.J. Turgot, "Réflexions sur la formation et la distribution des richesses," *Ephémérides du citoyen,* Nov. 1769-Jan. 1770. *Reflections on the Formation and the Distribution of Riches,* New York 1898.

4 A Fully Dynamic Setting: Neoclassical Full-Employment Growth

We that are young
Shall never see so much
Nor live so long.

William Shakespeare, *King Lear,* V, iii.

Until now we have used our dynamics sparingly. Chapter 3 introduced the bare minimum of it necessary to accomodate inflation, which was defined as a proportionate rate of growth.

But even if not so defined, other variables such as output, capital stock and its marginal productivity, the real wage rate, labor productivity, and the distributive shares deserve to be seen in their natural habitat, a growing economy. For a fully dynamic setting we choose Solow's (1956) well-known neoclassical growth model of a fully employed closed economy producing a single good from labor, an immortal capital stock of that good, and nothing else. Capital stock is the result of accumulated savings under an autonomously given propensity to consume. A production function permits substitution between labor and capital stock. In such a model let the money wage rate be growing autonomously, and let the price of goods adjust to it under profit maximization, pure competition, and autonomous technological progress.

Notation

Variables

C ≡ physical consumption
g_v ≡ proportionate rate of growth of variable $v ≡ x, P, S,$ and X
I ≡ physical investment
x ≡ physical marginal productivity of capital stock
L ≡ labor employed
P ≡ price of goods
S ≡ physical capital stock
W ≡ wage bill
X ≡ physical output
Y ≡ money income
Z ≡ profits bill

Parameters

a ≡ multiplicative factor of production function
a, β ≡ exponents of production function
c ≡ propensity to consume
F ≡ available labor force
g_v ≡ proportionate rate of growth of parameter $v \equiv a, F,$ and w
w ≡ money wage rate

All parameters are stationary except a, F, and w whose growth rates are stationary. Let us now specify the neoclassical growth model and solve for its steady–state equilibrium rates of growth.

The Neoclassical Growth Model

Definitions

Define the proportionate rate of growth

$$g_v \equiv \frac{dv}{dt}\frac{1}{v} \tag{4.1}$$

Define investment as the derivative of capital stock with respect to time:

$$I \equiv \frac{dS}{dt} \tag{4.2}$$

Production

Let entrepreneurs apply a Cobb–Douglas production function

$$X = aL^\alpha S^\beta \tag{4.3}$$

where $0 < \alpha < 1; 0 < \beta < 1; \alpha + \beta = 1$; and $a > 0$. Let profit maximization under pure competition equalize real wage rate and physical marginal productivity of labor:

$$\frac{w}{P} = \frac{\partial X}{\partial L} = \alpha \frac{X}{L} \tag{4.4}$$

Physical marginal productivity of capital stock is

$$\varkappa \equiv \frac{\partial X}{\partial S} = \beta \frac{X}{S} \tag{4.5}$$

Multiply by value of capital stock PS and define profits as

$$Z \equiv \varkappa PS = \beta PX \tag{4.6}$$

Employment

Assume the labor market to clear:

$$L = F \tag{4.7}$$

Define the wage bill as the money wage rate *times* employment:

$$W \equiv wL \tag{4.8}$$

National Money Income

Define national money income as the sum of wage and profits bill:

$$Y \equiv W + Z \tag{4.9}$$

Consumption Demand

Let consumption be a fixed proportion c of output:

$$C = cX \tag{4.10}$$

where $0 < c < 1$.

Goods-Market Equilibrium

Goods-market equilibrium requires the supply of goods to equal the demand for them:

$$X = C + I \tag{4.11}$$

Convergence to Steady-State Equilibrium Growth

To solve the system, insert equation 4.7 into 4.3 and differentiate with respect to time:

$$g_X = g_a + \alpha g_F + \beta g_S \tag{4.12}$$

Use equations 4.11, 4.10, 4.2, and 4.1 in that order to express the proportionate rate of growth of physical capital stock

$$g_S = (1 - c)X/S \tag{4.13}$$

Differentiate equation 4.13 with respect to time, use 4.1 and 4.12, and express the proportionate rate of acceleration of physical capital stock

$$g_{gS} = \alpha(g_a/\alpha + g_F - g_S) \tag{4.14}$$

In equation 4.14 there are three possibilities: if $g_S > g_a/\alpha + g_F$, then $g_{gS} < 0$. If

$$g_S = g_a/\alpha + g_F \tag{4.15}$$

then $g_{gS} = 0$. Finally, if $g_S < g_a/\alpha + g_F$, then $g_{gS} > 0$. Consequently, if greater than equation 4.15 g_S is falling; if equal to 4.15 g_S is stationary; and if less than 4.15 g_S is rising. Furthermore, g_S cannot alternate around 4.15, for differential equations trace continuous time paths, and as soon as a g_S-path touched 4.15 it would have to stay there. Finally, g_S cannot converge to anything else than 4.15, for if it did, by letting enough time elapse we could make the left-hand side of 4.14 smaller than any arbitrarily assignable positive constant ϵ, however small, without the same being possible for the right-hand side. We conclude that g_S must either equal $g_a/\alpha + g_F$ from the outset or, if it does not, converge to that value.

Insert equation 4.15 into 4.12 and find the growth rate of physical output

$$g_X = g_S \tag{4.16}$$

Differentiate equation 4.5 with respect to time, use 4.16, and find the growth rate of the physical marginal productivity of capital stock

$$g_x = 0 \tag{4.17}$$

Insert equation 4.7 into 4.4, differentiate the latter with respect to time, use equations 4.16 and 4.15, and find the rate of inflation

$$g_P = g_w - g_a/\alpha \tag{4.18}$$

That will be all we need to confront the neoclassical growth model with historical reality.

Reality and Neoclassical Growth

Convergence to Steady-State Growth of Output

As long as the growth rates g_a and g_F of technology and labor force, respectively, remain stationary, then according to our solutions 4.15 and 4.16 physical output should converge to a rising straight line in a semilogarithmic time diagram. Does it? Our figures 4-1 and 4-2 reproduce two diagrams by the U.S. Department of Commerce (1973: 97-98), showing seven real gross national products 1870-1970.

Between 1870 and 1969 the U.S. real gross national product was growing at an average annual rate of 0.037, and the first curve of figure 4-1 shows how. A kink is visible around 1910. The growth rate of the labor force is the net result of the birth, death, immigration, and participation rates, shown by the Department of Commerce (1973: 31, 42). Whether measured in man-hours (p. 25) or in number of men (p.29), a semilogarithmic U.S. labor force curve will display a conspicuous kink around 1910. That is the kink mirrored in the real gross national product curve of figure 4-1.

In the same period the West German real gross national product was growing at an average annual rate of 0.030. In 1945 the German economy lay in ruins. But in history's most perfect convergence the 1948-1969 West German curve in figure 4-1 swings back to an extrapolated 1870-1913 steady-state growth track! Japan, France, and Italy suffered severe war damage, too. In these countries postwar recovery was overshooting. The United Kingdom curve displays a kink around 1900: the economy failed to catch up with the second industrial revolution led by the United States and Germany.

Identical Steady-State Growth Rates
of Output and Capital Stock

If, as our solution 4.16 says, the growth rates of physical output and capital stock are the same, then in a time diagram the output-capital ratio X/S should appear as a horizontal line. Does it? Our figure 4-3 displays early findings by Denison (1962). Before 1930 and after 1945 the U.S. ratio X/S is roughly stationary. But there is a parallel upward shift in it between 1930 and 1945. The ratio should, and did, fall in the depressions of the early twenties and thirties: on short notice output can be pared down to demand but capital stock cannot. The ratio should rise in war, and did in the early forties: wide-

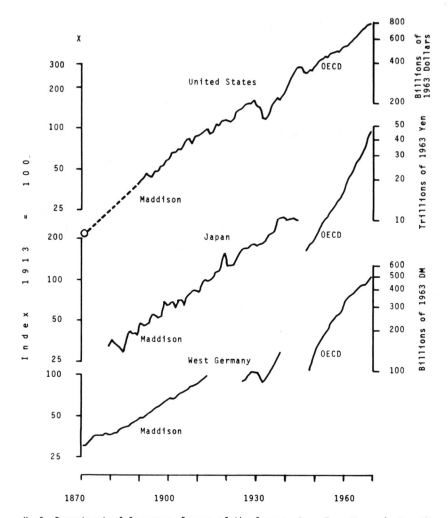

U. S. Department of Commerce, Bureau of the Census, *Long Term Economic Growth 1860–1970*, Washington, D. C., 1973, 97.

Figure 4–1. Gross National Product X, United States, Japan, and West Germany, 1870–1970

spread shift work allowed more output from the same capital stock. But the postwar ratio fell only part of the way back to its prewar level.

If we plot the growth rates of physical output and capital stock along the two axes of a diagram, then if equation 4.16 holds, all observations should lie on a 45° line. Do they? Our figure 4–4 displays findings by Kuznets (1971) for long periods and for a number of countries. Practically on the 45° line are Canada 1891–1926, Norway 1879–1899 as well as 1950–1962, the United

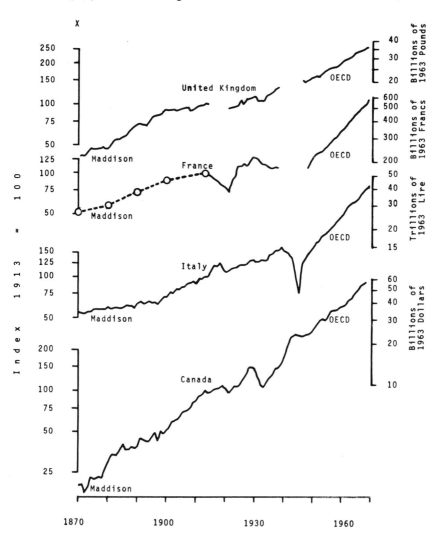

U. S. Department of Commerce, Bureau of the Census, *Long Term Economic Growth 1860-1970*, Washington, D. C., 1973, 98.

Figure 4-2. Gross National Product X, United Kingdom, France, Italy, and Canada, 1870–1970

Kingdom 1925/29–1963 as well as 1950–1962, and the United States 1889–1929. In 1950–1962 notice how war–torn economies like Germany and Italy are found high above the 45° line: once communications and power plants were destroyed, end–of–war output was negligible regardless of how much other plant and equipment was still standing. Modest early postwar reconstruction would then allow high rates of growth of output.

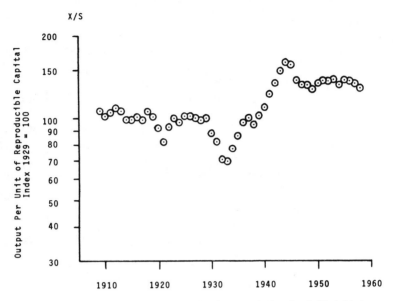

E. F. Denison, *The Sources of Economic Growth in the United States and the Alternatives Before Us*, New York, 1962.

Figure 4-3. The Output–Capital Ratio *X/S,* United States, 1909–1958

Stationary Rate of Return to Capital

In an immortal capital stock the physical marginal productivitiy x of capital stock represents the rate of return to capital. If, as our solution 4.17 says, the physical marginal productivity x of capital stock is growing at a zero rate, then in a time diagram the rate of return to capital should appear as a horizontal line. Does it? Our figure 4–5 displays findings by Kravis (1959) and Kendrick (1976). For the first half of the twentieth century Kravis calculated the ten–year moving averages shown in the upper half of figure 4–5. For the four decades 1929–1969 Kendrick calculated the cycle averages shown in the lower half. Kravis and Kendrick differed with respect to concepts, method, and scope. But they found roughly the same general level of return, the same trough of the Great Depression, and the same absence of any clear upward or downward trend.

Identical Steady–State Growth Rates of the Real Wage Rate and Labor Productivity

The real wage rate is *w/P,* hence its growth rate is $g_w - g_P$. Write our solution 4.18 as $g_w - g_P = g_a/\alpha$. Labor productivity is *X/L*; but according to

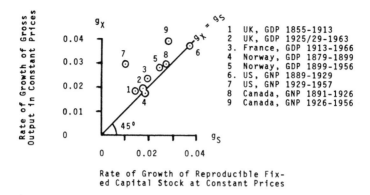

S. Kuznets, *Economic Growth of Nations, Total Output and Production Structure*, Cambridge, Mass., 1971, 74-75.

Figure 4-4. Growth Rates g_X and g_S of Output and Capital Stock, Respectively, Ten Countries, Longer and Shorter Runs

equation 4.7 $L = F$, hence the growth rate of labor productivity is $g_X - g_F$. Write our solutions 4.15 and 4.16 as $g_X - g_F = g_a/\alpha$. In other words, the growth rates of the real wage rate and labor productivity are the same. As long as g_a and α remain stationary, then, the real wage rate and labor produc-

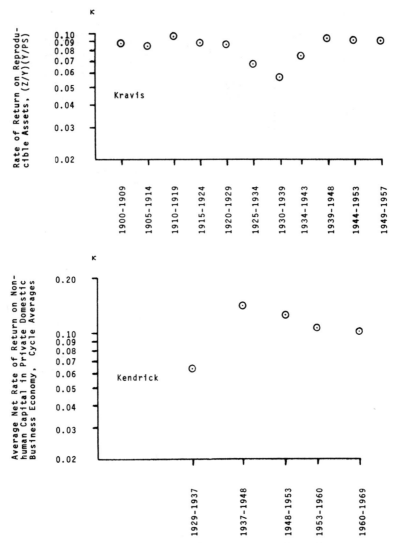

I. B. Kravis, "Relative Income Shares in Fact and Theory," *Amer. Econ. Rev.*, Dec. 1959, *49*, 938.

J. W. Kendrick assisted by Y. Lethem and J. Rowley, *The Formation and Stocks of Total Capital*, New York 1976, 124.

Figure 4-5. Rate of Return on Capital x, United States, 1900–1969

tivity expressed as index numbers should appear as two coinciding straight lines in a semilogarithmic time diagram. Do they? Our figures 4-6 and 4-7 reproduce two diagrams by Phelps Brown (1973), who found the real wage rate and labor productivity to have been growing as follows:

	$g_{w/P}$	$g_{X/L}$
United States 1890/99–1960	0.0208	0.0203
United Kingdom 1890/99–1960	0.0122	0.0083
Sweden 1892/99–1960	0.0191	0.0223
Germany 1890/99–1960	0.0161	0.0151

In the United States and Germany the correspondence between $g_{w/P}$ and $g_{X/L}$ is striking. In Sweden a divergence opens up around 1900, in the United Kingdom around 1950. The two divergences have opposite signs. Unionization seems to have little to do with them. Unionization has a large variance both in time and space. Britain, Germany, and Sweden became unionized at the turn of the century, the United States not until the thirties. In Sweden roughly 2/3 of all wage earners are unionized, in Britain 1/2, in Germany 1/3, and in the United States 1/5. But neither the different timing nor the different degree of unionization are readily apparent in figures 4–6 and 4–7.

Whatever, their causes, the opposite Swedish and United Kingdom divergences may have had important effects. A real wage rate lagging behind labor productivity will stimulate export and generate balance-of-trade surpluses—and did in Sweden in the period examined. A labor productivity lagging behind the real wage rate will impair export and generate balance-of-trade deficits—and did in the postwar United Kingdom.

Stationary Distributive Shares

Insert equation 4.4 into 4.8, equations 4.8 and 4.6 into 4.9, and find $Y = PX$ and the distributive shares $W/Y = \alpha$ and $Z/Y = \beta$. So the distributive shares should remain stationary. Did they?

For the United States Klein and Kosobud (1961) found labor's share to be the only one of their great ratios which was trendless. Kuznets (1966: 173) found the U.S. labor's share to have remained stationary from the turn of the century to the end of World War II. After that the share rose. Having imputed proprietors' income to labor and capital in the proportion applying to the rest of the economy, Kravis (1959), too, found a rising U.S. labor's share but found much of the rise to be a statistical illusion. As it appears in the national income accounts, income originating in goverment is by definition labor income—labor's share is one! Since in the postwar years government was a rising proportion of the economy, labor's share would be rising for that reason alone. Kravis suggested that "an alternative adjustment, and possibly a preferable one, is to exclude income originating in the government altogether." Our semilogarithmic figure 4–8 displays Kravis' findings before and after such exclusion.

For Sweden Jungenfelt (1966) found labor's share fluctuating around a stationary value of slightly above 0.70.

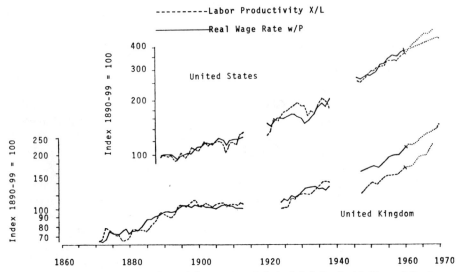

E. H. Phelps Brown, "Levels and Movements of Industrial Productivity and Real Wages Internationally Compared, 1860-1970," *Econ. J.*, Mar. 1973, *83*, 58-71.

Figure 4-6. Labor Productivity *X/L* and Real Wage Rate *w/P*, United States and United Kingdom, 1860–1970

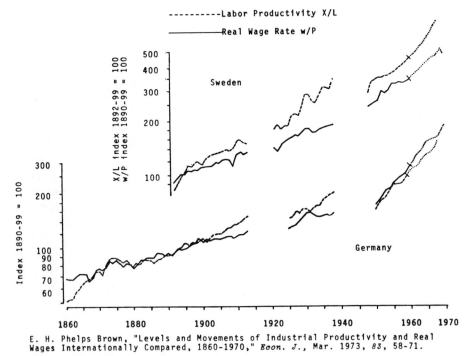

E. H. Phelps Brown, "Levels and Movements of Industrial Productivity and Real Wages Internationally Compared, 1860-1970," *Econ. J.*, Mar. 1973, *83*, 58-71.

Figure 4-7. Labor Productivity *X/L* and Real Wage Rate *w/P*, Sweden and Germany, 1860–1970

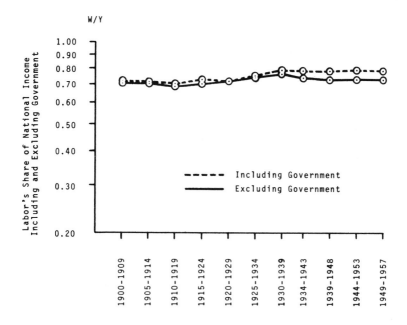

W/Y

I. B. Kravis, "Relative Income Shares in Fact and Theory," *Amer. Econ. Rev.*, Dec. 1959, *49*, 919 and 928.

Figure 4-8. Labor's Share *W/Y*, United States, 1900–1957

Denison examined labor's share both in time (1974) and space (1967). In his time series for the United States 1919-1968 he not only excluded government, as Kravis had done, but also income from investment abroad and dwellings. Proprietors' income was imputed to labor and capital by first assuming that proprietors were being paid the average wage rate of business employees and earning the same rate of return on their assets as were corporations. Then if the sum of such imputed income items exceeded actual proprietor's income (as it did in farming), all imputed income items were reduced in the proportion of actual to imputed income. Left with nonresidential business income, Denison calculated the U.S. shares displayed in the upper half of figure 4-9. They are practically stationary.

Equaling the exponents of the production function 4.3 the distributive shares should be the same wherever Western technology is applied. Are they? In his comparison of nine countries 1960-1962 Denison (1967) excluded income from investment abroad and dwellings, as in his time series. But he did not exclude government. The inclusion of government would be harmless if "the importance of the compensation of general government employees in 1960-62 was about the same in Northwest Europe as a whole, in Italy, and in the United States." Less harmless was the lack of European data

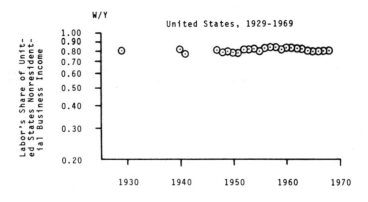

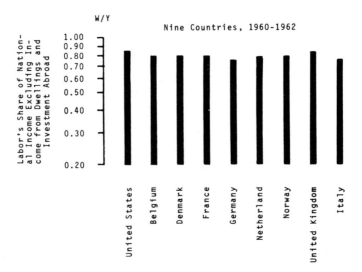

E. F. Denison, *Accounting for United States Economic Growth 1929-1969*, Washington, D. C., 1974, 260.

E. F. Denison, *Why Growth Rates Differ, Postwar Experience in Nine Western Countries*, Washington, D. C., 1967, 42.

Figure 4-9. Labor's Share *W/Y*, United States, 1929–1969, and Nine Countries, 1960–1962

which forced Denison to assume European proprietors' incomes to have the same labor's share as that calculated for the U.S. proprietors' income. With such hazards Denison calculated the shares displayed in the lower half of figure 4-9. They differ little among countries.

Conclusions

The solutions of the neoclassical growth model possessed five important properties: (1) convergence to steady-state growth of output, (2) identical steady-state growth rates of output and capital stock, (3) stationary rate of return to capital, (4) identical steady-state growth rates of the real wage rate and labor productivity, and (5) stationary distributive shares. We found none of the five properties to be seriously at odds with historical reality.

Let us compare the neoclassical full-employment growth model with its closest rival, the post-Keynesian one.

References

E.F. Denison, *The Sources of Economic Growth in the United States and the Alternatives Before Us,* New York 1962.

———, *Why Growth Rates Differ, Postwar Experience in Nine Western Countries,* Washington, D.C., 1967.

———, *Accounting for United States Economic Growth 1929-1969,* Washington, D.C., 1974.

K.G. Jungenfelt, *Löneandelen och den ekonomiska utvecklingen,* Stockholm 1966.

J.W. Kendrick assisted by Y. Lethem and J. Rowley, *The Formation and Stocks of Total Capital,* New York 1976.

L.R. Klein and R.F. Kosobud, "Some Econometrics of Growth: Great Ratios of Economics," *Quart. J. Econ.,* May 1961, *75,* 173-198.

I.B. Kravis, "Relative Income Shares in Fact and Theory," *Amer. Econ. Rev.,* Dec. 1959, *49,* 917-949.

S. Kuznets, *Modern Economic Growth, Rate, Structure and Spread,* New Haven 1966.

———, *Economic Growth of Nations, Total Output and Production Structure,* Cambridge, Mass., 1971.

E.H. Phelps Brown, "Levels and Movements of Industrial Productivity and Real Wages Internationally Compared, 1860-1970," *Econ. J.,* Mar. 1973, *83,* 58-71.

R.M. Solow, "A Contribution to the Theory of Economic Growth," *Quart. J. Econ.,* Feb. 1956, *70,* 65-94.

U.S. Department of Commerce, Bureau of the Census, *Long Term Economic Growth 1860-1970,* Washington, D.C., 1973.

5 Neoclassicals and Post-Keynesians: Alternative Theories of Distribution

The whole dispute between Keynesian and non-Keynesian theories is whether investment determines savings, or vice versa. Nicholas Kaldor (1966)

Let us identify similarities and dissimilarities between neoclassicals and post-Keynesians and ask four specific questions. First, does saving or investment adjust to a higher propensity to save, and how? Second, within that adjustment, what are the roles played by income distribution, the real wage rate, and mark-up pricing? Third, within that adjustment, does a Wicksell effect emerge? Fourth, are the models examined open or closed and if closed, how? We specify both models in their stripped form and in the same notation.

Notation

Variables

$C \equiv$ physical consumption
$g_v \equiv$ proportionate rate of growth of variable $v \equiv S$ and X
$I \equiv$ physical investment
$\varkappa \equiv$ physical marginal productivity of capital stock
$L \equiv$ labor employed
$P \equiv$ price of good
$S \equiv$ physical capital stock
$W \equiv$ wage bill
$X \equiv$ physical output
$Y \equiv$ money income
$Z \equiv$ profits bill
$z \equiv$ mark-up pricing factor

Parameters

$a, b \equiv$ multiplicative factors of production functions
$\alpha, \beta \equiv$ exponents of Cobb-Douglas production function
$c \equiv$ propensity to consume
$F \equiv$ available labor force

g_v ≡ proportionate rate of growth of parameter $v ≡ F$
w ≡ money wage rate

Equations Common to Both Models

We confine ourselves to the stripped form of either model having one good, an immortal capital stock of that good, and no technological progress in it. Four definitions and one equilibrium condition are common to both models. Define the proportionate rate of growth

$$g_v \equiv \frac{dv}{dt}\frac{1}{v} \tag{5.1}$$

Define investment as the derivative of capital stock with respect to time:

$$I \equiv \frac{dS}{dt} \tag{5.2}$$

Define the wage bill as the money wage rate *times* employment:

$$W \equiv wL \tag{5.3}$$

Define national money income as the sum of wage and profits bill:

$$Y \equiv W + Z \tag{5.4}$$

Market equilibrium requires the supply of goods to equal the demand for them:

$$X = C + I \tag{5.5}$$

Equations Peculiar to the Neoclassical Model

Production

Let entrepreneurs apply a Cobb–Douglas production function

$$X = aL^{\alpha}S^{\beta} \tag{5.6}$$

where $0 < \alpha < 1; 0 < \beta < 1; \alpha + \beta = 1;$ and $a > 0$. Let profit maximization under pure competition equalize real wage rate and physical marginal productivity of labor:

$$\frac{w}{P} = \frac{\partial X}{\partial L} = \alpha \frac{X}{L} \tag{5.7}$$

Physical marginal productivity of capital stock is

$$\varkappa \equiv \frac{\partial X}{\partial S} = \beta \frac{X}{S} \tag{5.8}$$

Multiply by value of capital stock PS and define profits as

$$Z \equiv \varkappa PS = \beta PX \tag{5.9}$$

Assume full employment:

$$L = F \tag{5.10}$$

Distributive Shares

Insert equation 5.7 into 5.3, equations 5.3 and 5.9 into 5.4, and find $Y = PX$ and the distributive shares $W/Y = \alpha$ and $Z/Y = \beta$. Notice that we derived this result before specifying our neoclassical consumption function

$$C = cX \tag{5.11}$$

where $0 < c < 1$. In the distributive shares, then, the form of the consumption function makes no difference. For example, the latter may well be a post–Keynesian one like equation 5.18 below with realistic different propensities c_w and c_z to consume real wages and profits, respectively. In that case we simply have $c \equiv \alpha c_w + \beta c_z$.

Does Saving or Investment Adjust to a
Higher Propensity to Save?

If the propensity to save $1 - c$ were twice as high, how would a neoclassical model adjust? The adjustment would begin with a typical response of factor proportion to relative factor price. Divide equation 5.6 by L and 5.7 by α and set the resulting expressions for X/L equal. Find

$$S/L = (\alpha a)^{-1/\beta} (w/P)^{1/\beta} \tag{5.12}$$

So a higher real wage rate w/P would induce a higher capital intensity S/L. But what would the real wage rate be?

The Real Wage Rate and the Wicksell Effect

To solve for the real wage rate divide equation 5.6 by S, raise both sides to the power -1, and find the capital coefficient: $S/X = (1/a)(S/L)^{\alpha}$.

Next use equations 5.1 and 5.2 to write $I \equiv g_S S$, insert that and 5.11 into 5.5, and find another expression for the capital coefficient

$$S/X = (1 - c)/g_S \qquad (5.13)$$

Finally set the right-hand sides of the two expressions for S/X equal, insert the result into equation 5.12, and find the real wage rate

$$w/P = \alpha a^{1/\alpha}[(1 - c)/g_S]^{\beta/\alpha} \qquad (5.14)$$

Here is the Wicksell effect: according to equation 5.14, the real wage rate w/P is the higher the higher is the propensity to save $1 - c$ or, as Wicksell (1934: 164) expressed his effect: "The capitalist saver is, thus, fundamentally, the friend of labour."

Closing the Neoclassical Model

Equation 5.14 is not a solution yet. So far it merely expresses one unknown, the real wage rate w/P, in terms of another, the rate of growth of capital stock g_S. But neoclassicists do close their models. In the absence of technological progress they find proportionate rates of growth to be converging to the steady–state solutions

$$g_S = g_X = g_F \qquad (5.15)$$

Insert equation 5.15 into 5.14, and you have a neoclassical solution for the real wage rate w/P.

The full adjustment mechanism is now visible. According to 5.14 with 5.15 inserted, an economy with twice the propensity to save will have a $2^{\beta/\alpha}$ times higher real wage rate which will induce a $2^{(\beta/\alpha)(1/\beta)} = 2^{1/\alpha}$ times higher capital intensity which means a $2^{(\beta/\alpha)(1/\beta)\alpha} = 2$ times higher capital coefficient. Summing up: according to equation 5.13, the economy with twice the overall propensity to save will have a capital coefficient twice as high.

This result may be illustrated graphically: write equation 5.13 as $g_S S/X = 1 - c$.

Here the left-hand side is the investment ratio and is in direct proportion to the capital coefficient S/X, hence must appear in figure 5-1 as a

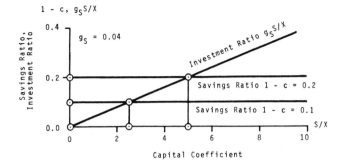

Figure 5-1. The Capital Coefficient S/X as the Equilibrating Variable in a Neoclassical Savings–Investment Equilibrium

straight line through the origin with the slope g_S. The right-hand side is the savings ratio and is a parameter, hence must appear in figure 5-1 as a horizontal line. The abscissa of the intersection point between the investment-ratio line and the savings-ratio line is the equilibrium value of the capital coefficient: the economy with twice the overall propensity to save will have a capital coefficient twice as high.

Equations Peculiar to Post–Keynesian Models

Production

A post-Keynesian model has fixed input-output coefficients:

$$L = aX \tag{5.16}$$

$$S = bX \tag{5.17}$$

Two facts are readily apparent. First, there can be no response of factor proportion to relative factor price, for according to equation 5.16 and 5.17 the factor proportion is $S/L = b/a$, a parameter. Second, 5.16 and 5.17 are a simultaneous system implying simultaneous variation of L and S with X. Taking partial derivatives of X with respect to L or S is therefore impossible. Marginal productivities are such partial derivatives. Consequently, to find their distributive shares post-Keynesians need something else than marginal productivities.

Distributive Shares

The simplest form of a post–Keynesian model has a propensity to consume wages equaling one. In that case the consumption function is

$$C = W/P + c_Z Z/P \qquad (5.18)$$

With immortal capital stock, the entire value of national output represents value added, that is, national money income

$$Y \equiv PX \qquad (5.19)$$

Insert equation 5.4 into 5.19, divide by P, and write

$$X \equiv W/P + Z/P \qquad (5.20)$$

Subtract equation 5.18 from 5.20 and insert 5.5. Use equations 5.1 and 5.2 to write $I \equiv g_S S$, insert 5.17 into that, divide by X, and use 5.19 to find the profits share

$$Z/Y = bg_S /(1 - c_Z) \qquad (5.21)$$

Closing the Post–Keynesian Model

Equation 5.21 is not a solution yet. So far it merely expresses one unknown, the profits share Z/Y, in terms of another, the rate of growth of capital stock g_S. Do post-Keynesians close their system? At this point Kaldorian (1957; 1966) and Robinsonian (1956; 1971) ways are parting.

Kaldor considers the rate of growth of capital stock g_S a variable and solves for it by assuming full employment, as neoclassicists do. Insert equation 5.10 into 5.16, take the derivatives of 5.16 and 5.17 with respect to time, use 5.1, and find that in the absence of technological progress steady-state proportionate rates of growth are equation 5.15: $g_S = g_X = g_F$.

Insert 5.15 into 5.21, and you have a Kaldorian solution for the profits share Z/Y.

But to Joan Robinson, g_S is autonomously given by the "animal spirits" of nonprofit-maximizing and otherwise nonrational entrepreneurs. So 5.21 is already a Robinsonian solution for the profits share.

Does Saving or Investment Adjust to a Higher Propensity to Save?

If the parametric propensity to save real profits $1 - c_Z$ were twice as high, how would the post-Keynesian model adjust? Let us read equation 5.21 as follows. If two economies have the same capital coefficient b and are growing at the same proportionate rate g_S, but one economy has a propensity to save real profits $1 - c_Z$ twice as high as that of the other economy, then the former economy will have a profits share Z/Y half that of the latter.

This result, too, may be illustrated graphically: write equation 5.21 as

$$(1 - c_Z)Z/Y = bg_S.$$

Here the left-hand side is the savings ratio and is in direct proportion to the profits share Z/Y, hence must appear in figure 5-2 as a straight line through the origin with the slope $1 - c_Z$. The right-hand side is the investment ratio and is—with equation 5.15 inserted—a parameter, hence must appear in figure 5-2 as a horizontal line. The abscissa of the intersection point between the savings-ratio line and the investment-ratio line is the equilibrium value of the profits share. The economy with twice the propensity to save real profits will have half the profits share.

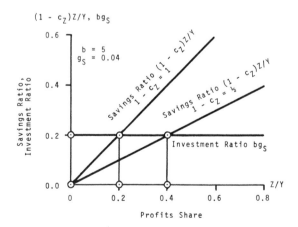

Figure 5-2. The Profits Share Z/Y as the Equilibrating Variable in a Post-Keynesian Savings-Investment Equilibrium

The Real Wage Rate, Mark-up Pricing,
and a Wicksell Effect?

In the post-Keynesian model the real wage rate is hiding behind a pricing formula that in "modern manufacturing industry ... prices are formed by adding a margin to prime cost," as Joan Robinson (1971) expresses it in her postscript. In a one-good post-Keynesian model "prime cost" is labor cost only, and according to equation 5.16 per-unit labor cost is aw, hence the formula for price P is $P = awz$ and for the real wage rate

$$w/P = 1/(az) \qquad (5.22)$$

where z is the mark-up factor, and $z > 1$.

Mark-up pricing may be a deviation from neoclassical language but not from neoclassical substance. Under neoclassical pure competition, too, there are overhead costs to be covered, and freedom of entry and exit will see to it that they are, so neoclassical price, too, will exceed prime cost. The proportion in which it does is easily found: write equation 5.7 as

$$P = \frac{w}{\alpha}\, \frac{L}{X} \qquad (5.7)$$

or in English: price P exceeds per-unit labor cost wL/X in the proportion $1/\alpha$. Since $0 < \alpha < 1$, the neoclassical "mark-up" factor $1/\alpha > 1$.

But isn't the post-Keynesian mark-up factor z an interesting new structural parameter reflecting "the degree of monopoly"? If it were, Joan Robinson's system would be overdetermined: divide equation 5.4 by Y, insert 5.3, 5.16, 5.19, and 5.22, and find another expression for the profits share:

$$Z/Y = 1 - 1/z \qquad (5.23)$$

Consider our two expressions for the profits share 5.21—if Kaldorian, with 5.15 inserted—and 5.23. If z were a parameter, those expressions would be two equations in *one* unknown Z/Y, hence would represent an overdetermined system. If z were a variable, those expressions would be two equations in the *two* unknowns Z/Y and z, and we could solve for z:

$$z = 1/[1 - bg_S/(1 - c_Z)] \qquad (5.24)$$

So we have found the post-Keynesian mark-up factor z to be merely another variable inherent in the savings-investment adjustment mechanism: Joan Robinson's rate of growth of capital stock g_S was given exogenously by the "animal spirits" of entrepreneurs. Thus Robinsonian entrepreneurs may take their pick: choosing a lower g_S would reduce the profits share 5.21, would lower the mark-up factor 5.24 and thereby raise the real wage rate 5.22.

Do post-Keynesian models have a Wicksell effect? We might expect none but find one just the same: a higher propensity to save real profits $1 - c_Z$ would reduce the profits share 5.21, lower the mark-up factor 5.24 and thereby raise the real wage rate 5.22. Even a Robinsonian capitalist is "fundamentally the friend of labour."

Conclusions

This chapter has tried to answer four questions. First, is Kaldor correct in saying that in neoclassical models savings determine investment whereas in post-Keynesian models investment determines savings? Taken literally, he is wrong: savings and investment are both variables determined simultaneously by the parameters of the system. A correctly asked question would be: how sensitive are they to those parameters? What Kaldor really means is that neoclassical and post-Keynesian models have very different sensitivities to the parametric propensity to save. In the neoclassical model, doubling that propensity was found to double the capital coefficient—something on the investment side. In the post-Keynesian model, doubling the propensity was found to halve the profits share—something on the savings side.

Second, is the post-Keynesian mark-up factor an interesting new structural parameter reflecting "the degree of monopoly"? Our answer was No: we found it to be merely another variable inherent in the savings-investment adjustment mechanism.

Third, will a Wicksell effect emerge? We found an expected one in the neoclassical model and a perhaps unexpected one in the post-Keynesian model.

Fourth, are the models examined open or closed? Yes and no! Kaldor's profit share is determined by his full-employment assumption requiring capital stock, output, and available labor force to be growing at the same rate 5.15. As Tobin (1959-1960) pointed out, the Kaldorian system may be special, arbitrary, and rigid. The burden of adjustment it imposes upon the distributive shares may be heavy, and the distributive shares of the real world may not actually be carrying such a burden; the capital coefficient is more likely to be carrying it. Among the few advanced economies offering usable data on such things, the capital coefficient seems to vary more than do the distributive shares. The United States 1953-1969 had a net propensity to save of 0.081 and a capital coefficient of 2.28; compare Brems (1973:

35). Both are roughly one-half of their Swedish counterparts: Sweden, according to Lindbeck (1972: 172), has a net propensity to save of 0.14 and according to Lundberg (1961: 111), a capital coefficient of 4 to 5, but according to Jungenfelt (1966), a labor's share of 0.70—much like that of the United States.

Still, at least the Kaldorian system is a closed one. By contrast, Joan Robinson's system is an open one. Her profits share as well as her mark-up factor are determined by letting nonprofit-maximizing and otherwise non-rational entrepreneurs fix an arbitrary growth rate of capital stock. Analytical economists consider such openness a deficiency. But perhaps the very openness appeals to interventionists: control that growth rate and you control income distribution! Perhaps, then, the appeal of post-Keynesian distribution theory is ideological rather than analytical; neoclassical theory is more flexible and has less to fear from confrontation with the real world; compare chapter 4.

The following chapters modify, extend, and apply the neoclassical growth model to simultaneous unemployment and inflation, to a corporate economy, to mortal capital stock, to exhaustible and nonexhaustible natural resources, to two goods, and to two countries.

References

H. Brems, *Labor, Capital, and Growth,* Lexington, Mass. 1973.
———, "Reality and Neoclassical Theory," *J. Econ. Lit.,* March 1977, *15,* 72–83.
K.G. Jungenfelt, *Löneandelen och den ekonomiska utvecklingen,* Stockholm 1966.
N. Kaldor, "A Model of Economic Growth," *Econ. J.,* Dec. 1957, *67,* 591–624.
———, "Marginal Productivity and Macroeconomic Theories of Distribution," *Rev. Econ. Stud.,* 1966, *33,* 309–319.
A. Lindbeck, *Swedish Economic Policy,* Berkeley and Los Angeles 1972.
E. Lundberg, *Produktivitet och räntabilitet,* Stockholm 1961.
J. Robinson, *The Accumulation of Capital,* London 1956.
———, "Solow on the Rate of Return," in G.C. Harcourt and N.F. Laing (eds.), *Capital and Growth,* Baltimore, Md. 1971, 168–179.
R.M. Solow, "A Contribution to the Theory of Economic Growth," *Quart. J. Econ.,* Feb. 1956, *70,* 65–94.
J. Tobin, "Towards a *General* Kaldorian Theory of Distribution," *Rev. Econ. Stud.,* 1959–1960, *27,* 119–120.
K. Wicksell, *Föreläsningar i nationalekonomi I,* Lund 1901, translated *Lectures on Political Economy I,* London 1934.

Could Wicksell, Keynes, and Monetarists Coexist in Neoclassical Growth?

The purpose of this chapter is to open the neoclassical growth model to unemployment and inflation. In two respects we shall modify the standard Solow (1956) neoclassical growth model set out in chapter 4.

First, our labor market will not be assumed to clear. But let there be a price equation derived from profit maximization and including the wage expectations of the entrepreneurs. Let there be a wage equation representing a Phillips function and including the price expectations of labor. Let a price-wage equilibrium be defined as self-fulfilling expectations. We shall examine the existence and the properties of such an equilibrium.

Second, we shall need a bare minimum of monetary arrangements. Let there be a money market in which firms may borrow by selling interest-bearing claims upon themselves. Such claims are bought by savers and monetary authorities alike. The monetary authorities may expand their stock of claims, and with it the money supply, more or less rapidly. The pace at which they expand it will affect the yield of the claims. Let the nominal rate of interest be defined as that yield.

Notation

Variables

$C \equiv$ physical consumption
$D \equiv$ demand for money
$g_v \equiv$ proportionate rate of growth of variable $v \equiv C, D, I, \varkappa, L, M, P, r, \varrho,$ $S, w, X,$ and Y
$I \equiv$ physical investment
$k \equiv$ present gross worth of another physical unit of capital stock
$\varkappa \equiv$ physical marginal productivity of capital stock
$L \equiv$ labor employed
$\lambda \equiv$ proportion employed of available labor force
$M \equiv$ supply of money
$N \equiv$ present net worth of entire physical capital stock
$n \equiv$ present net worth of another physical unit of capital stock
$P \equiv$ price of goods
$p \equiv$ one coefficient of Phillips function representing inflationary potential

r ≡ nominal rate of interest
ϱ ≡ real rate of interest
S ≡ physical capital stock
w ≡ money wage rate
X ≡ physical output
Y ≡ money income

Parameters

a ≡ multiplicative factor of production function
$\alpha, \beta,$ ≡ exponents of production function
c ≡ propensity to consume
F ≡ available labor force
g_v ≡ proportionate rate of growth of parameter $v \equiv a$ and F
m ≡ multiplicative factor of demand for money function
μ ≡ exponent of demand for money function
π ≡ exponent of Phillips function
Φ ≡ another coefficient of Phillips function

All parameters are stationary except a and F whose growth rates are stationary. Let us now specify our modified neoclassical growth model.

A Modified Neoclassical Growth Model

Definitions

Define the proportionate rate of growth

$$g_v \equiv \frac{dv}{dt}\frac{1}{v} \tag{6.1}$$

Define investment as the derivative of capital stock with respect to time:

$$I \equiv \frac{dS}{dt} \tag{6.2}$$

Production and the Price Equation

Let entrepreneurs apply a Cobb–Douglas production function

$$X = aL^{\alpha}S^{\beta} \tag{6.3}$$

where $0 < \alpha < 1; 0 < \beta < 1; \alpha + \beta = 1;$ and $a > 0$. Let profit mazimization under pure competition equalize real wage rate and physical marginal productivity of labor:

$$\frac{w}{P} = \frac{\partial X}{\partial L} = \alpha \frac{X}{L} \qquad (6.4)$$

Write equation 6.4 as

$$P = \frac{w}{\alpha} \frac{L}{X}$$

used in chapter 5 to demonstrate that the neoclassical model has mark-up pricing, too: neoclassical price P exceeds per-unit labor cost wL/X in the proportion $1/\alpha$. Differentiate this form of equation 6.4 with respect to time and find

$$g_P = g_w + g_L - g_X \qquad (6.5)$$

telling us that, given their expectations of the rates of growth of the money wage rate g_w and of per-unit labor input $g_L - g_X$, entrepreneurs will charge a price growing at the rate 6.5. Our price equation has empirical support: in their price equation Eckstein and Girola (1978: 328) found no room for demand represented by, say, the rate of unemployment; "actual prices stay near equilibrium and trace out the cost curves."

Physical marginal productivity of capital stock is

$$\varkappa \equiv \frac{\partial X}{\partial S} = \beta \frac{X}{S} \qquad (6.6)$$

Investment Demand

Let N be the present net worth of new capital stock S installed by an entrepreneur. Let his desired capital stock be the size of stock maximizing present net worth. A first-order condition for a maximum is

$$n \equiv \frac{\partial N}{\partial S} = 0 \qquad (6.7)$$

To find desired capital stock proceed as follows. Let entrepreneurs be purely competitive ones, then price P of output is beyond their control. At time t, therefore, marginal value productivity of capital stock is $\varkappa(t)P(t)$. As seen from the present time τ marginal value productivity at time t is

$\varkappa(t)P(t)e^{-r(t-\tau)}$, where r is the stationary nominal rate of interest used as a discount rate. Define present gross worth of another physical unit of capital stock as the present worth of all future marginal value productivities over its entire useful life:

$$k(\tau) \equiv \int_{\tau}^{\infty} \varkappa(t)P(t)e^{-r(t-\tau)}dt \qquad (6.8)$$

Let entrepreneurs expect physical marginal productivity of capital stock to be growing at the stationary rate g_x:

$$\varkappa(t) = \varkappa(\tau)e^{g_x(t-\tau)} \qquad (6.9)$$

and price of output to be growing at the stationary rate g_P:

$$P(t) = P(\tau)e^{g_P(t-\tau)} \qquad (6.10)$$

Insert equations 6.9 and 6.10 into 6.8, define

$$\varrho \equiv r - (g_x + g_P) \qquad (6.11)$$

and write the integral 6.8 as

$$k(\tau) = \int_{\tau}^{\infty} \varkappa(\tau)P(\tau)e^{-\varrho(t-\tau)}dt$$

Neither $\varkappa(\tau)$ nor $P(\tau)$ is a function of t, hence may be taken outside the integral sign. Our g_x, g_P, and r were all said to be stationary, hence the coefficient ϱ of t is stationary, too. Assume $\varrho > 0$. As a result, find the integral to be

$$k = \varkappa P/\varrho \qquad (6.12)$$

Find present net worth of another physical unit of capital stock as its gross worth *minus* its price:

$$n \equiv k - P = (\varkappa/\varrho - 1)P \qquad (6.13)$$

Applying our first-order condition 6.7 to our result 6.13, find equilibrium physical marginal productivity of capital stock

$$\varkappa = \varrho \qquad (6.14)$$

Finally take equations 6.6 and 6.14 together and find desired capital stock

$$S = \beta X/\varrho \qquad (6.15)$$

Apply definitions 6.1 and 6.2 to equation 6.15 and find desired investment as the derivative of desired capital stock with respect to time:

$$I \equiv \frac{dS}{dt} = \beta g_x X / \varrho \qquad (6.16)$$

Equations 6.15 and 6.16 are capital stock and investment desired by an individual entrepreneur. Except X everything on the right-hand side of 6.15 and 6.16 is common to all entrepreneurs. Factor out all common factors, sum over all entrepreneurs, then X becomes national output, and 6.15 and 6.16 become national desired capital stock and investment. So desired investment is in direct proportion to the elasticity β of output with respect to capital stock, the rate of growth g_x of output, and output X itself. Desired investment is in inverse proportion to ϱ. As we shall see below, ϱ is the real rate of interest. Our investment function 6.16 neatly encompasses Wicksellian, Keynesian, monetarist, and post-Keynesian ideas.

Wicksellian, Keynesian, Monetarist,
and Post-Keynesian Investment

Wicksell (1935: 193) defined a rate of interest which would equal the "expected yield on the newly created capital" and called it a "natural" rate. Keynes (1936: 135) defined the same thing but called it the "marginal efficiency of capital." Wicksell and Keynes would have agreed with our equation 6.14 that "new investment will be pushed to the point at which the marginal efficiency of capital becomes equal to the rate of interest," Keynes (1936: 184). But as we saw in chapters 1 and 2, neither Wicksell nor Keynes distinguished between a nominal and a real rate of interest.

Monetarists like Turgot (1898: 49), Fisher (1896: 8-9), and Mundell (1971) did distinguish: investment would not be lower just because the nominal rate of interest were higher; only "an increase in the real interest rate lowers investment," Mundell (1971: 16).

Given an incremental capital coefficient b, post-Keynesians like Harrod (1948) determine desired investment as $I = bdX/dt \equiv bg_x X$. As in equation 6.16, investment is in direct proportion to the rate of growth of output and to output itself.

Consumption Demand

Let consumption be a fixed proportion c of output:

$$C = cX \qquad (6.17)$$

where $0 < c < 1$.

Goods–Market Equilibrium

Goods–market equilibrium requires the supply of goods to equal the demand for them:

$$X = C + I \tag{6.18}$$

Employment, the Phillips Function
and the Wage Equation

Let labor employed be the proportion λ of available labor force:

$$L = \lambda F \tag{6.19}$$

where $0 < \lambda < 1$, and λ is so far not a function of time.

Within their province but tempered by unemployment, labor unions according to Phillips (1958) will seek a relative gain by raising the money wage rate.

The original Phillips curve had no room for labor's inflationary expectations. But knowing that the gain would merely be temporary would not keep labor from seeking it; on the contrary, by expecting inflation labor would be compelled to contribute to it. And in their empirical wage equation Eckstein and Girola (1978: 325–327), found unemployment and current inflation to be the "bulk of the explanation." We write a modern Phillips function by subtracting employment 6.19 from available labor force F, finding the unemployment fraction to be $1 - \lambda$, and incorporating labor's inflationary expectations g_P:

$$g_w = p(1 - \lambda)^\pi + \Phi g_P \tag{6.20}$$

where $\Phi \geq 0$, $\pi < 0$, and $p > 0$ and so far not a function of time. Our wage equation 6.20 tells us that, given its expectations of the rate of growth of price g_P, labor will seek a money wage rate growing at the rate 6.20.

National Money Income

With immortal capital stock the entire value of national output represents value added, that is, national money income

$$Y \equiv PX \tag{6.21}$$

Money

Let the demand for money be a function of national money income and the nominal rate of interest:

$$D = mYr^{\mu} \qquad (6.22)$$

where $\mu < 0$ and $m > 0$.

Money-Market Equilibrium

Money-market equilibrium requires the supply of money to equal the demand for it:

$$M = D \qquad (6.23)$$

Let us prove Solow convergence.

Convergence to Steady-State Equilibrium Growth

Our modified neoclassical growth model includes all the equations needed to duplicate the Solow convergence proof of chapter 4. Insert equation 6.19, where λ is so far not a function of time, into our production function 6.3, differentiate the latter with respect to time, and express the proportionate rate of growth of physical output: $g_X = g_a + \alpha g_F + \beta g_S$, which is identical to equation 4.12. Use equations 6.18, 6.17, 6.2, and 6.1 in that order to express the proportionate rate of growth of physical capital stock: $g_S = (1 - c)X/S$, which is identical to equation 4.13. Differentiate with respect to time and express the proportionate rate of acceleration of physical capital stock: $g_{gS} = \alpha(g_a/\alpha + g_F - g_S)$, which is identical to equation 4.14. Here there are three possibilities: if $g_S > g_a/\alpha + g_F$, then $g_{gS} < 0$. If $g_S = g_a/\alpha + g_F$, then $g_{gS} = 0$. Finally, if $g_S < g_a/\alpha + g_F$, then $g_{gS} > 0$. Furthermore, as shown in chapter 4, g_S can neither alternate around $g_a/\alpha + g_F$ nor converge to anything else. We conclude that g_S must either equal $g_a/\alpha + g_F$ or, if it does not, converge to that value.

Our convergence proof will help us solve our model for its steady-state equilibrium rates of growth and interest.

**Steady–State Equilibrium Growth–Rate
and Interest–Rate Solutions**

Steady–State Growth

By taking derivatives with respect to time of all equations involving the thirteen variables C, D, I, $\varkappa$, L, M, P, r, ϱ, S, w, X, and Y, the reader may convince himself that the system 6.1 through 6.23 is satisfied by the following steady–state growth–rate solutions:

$$g_C = g_X \tag{6.24}$$

$$g_D = g_M \tag{6.25}$$

$$g_I = g_X \tag{6.26}$$

$$g_\varkappa = g_X - g_S \tag{6.27}$$

$$g_L = g_F \tag{6.28}$$

$$g_M = g_Y \tag{6.29}$$

$$g_P = \frac{p(1 - \lambda)^\pi - g_a/\alpha}{1 - \Phi} \tag{6.30}$$

$$g_r = 0 \tag{6.31}$$

$$g_\varrho = 0 \tag{6.32}$$

$$g_S = g_X \tag{6.33}$$

$$g_w = \frac{p(1 - \lambda)^\pi - \Phi g_a/\alpha}{1 - \Phi} \tag{6.34}$$

$$g_X = g_a/\alpha + g_F \tag{6.35}$$

$$g_Y = g_F + g_w \tag{6.36}$$

Our growth was steady-state growth, for no right-hand side of our solutions 6.24 through 6.36 was a function of time—the employment fraction λ and the coefficient p were assumed not to be.

Rates of Interest

Wicksell (1935: 193, 201) defined a rate of interest which would equilibrate saving with investment and called it a "normal" rate. Keynes (1930) defined the same rate but called it a "natural" one. Our own system meets that condition: insert equation 6.17 into 6.18 and find

$$(1 - c)X = I \tag{6.37}$$

Keynes (1936: 167) defined a rate of interest which would equilibrate the available quantity of cash with the desire to hold it. Our equation 6.23 shows that our own system meets that condition, too. But unlike the Wicksellian and Keynesian systems, our system has two interest rates. Its real rate of interest is found by inserting solutions 6.27 and 6.33 into our definition 6.11:

$$\varrho = r - g_P \tag{6.38}$$

To solve for ϱ insert equation 6.16 into 6.37, assume nonzero physical output X, divide X away, and find

$$\varrho = \beta g_X/(1 - c) \tag{6.39}$$

where g_X stands for our solution 6.35. The properties of equation 6.39 are quite Fisherian. In a thrifty economy the low c will make the real rate of interest ϱ low: "Where, as in Scotland, there are educational tendencies which instill the habit of thrift from childhood, the rate of interest tends to be low," Fisher (1930: 478). In a rapidly growing economy the high g_X will make the real rate of interest ϱ high: "the constant stream of new inventions, by making the available income streams rich in the future, at the sacrifice of immediate income, tends to make the rate of interest high," Fisher (1930: 481). Insert equation 6.39 into 6.38 and find the nominal rate of interest

$$r = \beta g_X/(1 - c) + g_P \tag{6.40}$$

where g_P and g_X stand for solutions 6.30 and 6.35, respectively. Insert equation 6.34 into 6.36 and 6.36 into 6.29 and find the rate of growth of the money supply which would uphold 6.39 and 6.40:

$$g_M = g_F + [p(1 - \lambda)^\tau - \Phi g_a/\alpha]/(1 - \Phi) \tag{6.41}$$

Self-fulfilling Expectations

Our system implies self-fulfilling expectations: we used the same symbol for the expected and realized values of any variable, implying equality between the two. Is such equality always possible? Yes, if the system has a set of solutions. It had the set 6.24 through 6.41.

Consequently our price-wage equilibrium implies, first, that if entrepreneurs expect labor to adopt the solution value 6.34 of the rate of growth of the money wage rate, then the entrepreneurs will adopt the solution value 6.30 of the rate of growth of price. Second, if labor expects entrepreneurs to do so, then labor will adopt the solution value 6.34 of the rate of growth of the money wage rate.

Infinitely Many Solutions

Our system has infinitely many solutions, that is, for a given employment fraction λ one for each value of the coefficient p, and for each value of the coefficient p one for each employment fraction λ.

But what if instead of being considered a variable, the rate of growth g_M of the money supply were considered a policy parameter controlled by the monetary authorities? Write equation 6.41 as

$$p(1 - \lambda)^\tau = (1 - \Phi)(g_M - g_F) + \Phi g_a /\alpha \qquad (6.41)$$

Here, if g_M were a parameter, there would be nothing but parameters on the right-hand side, and the product $p(1 - \lambda)^\tau$ would be determined. Would this mean that the employment fraction λ and the coefficient p would be what the monetary authorities allowed them to be? Would it mean that the monetary authorities could choose an attractive pair of, say, a high λ and a low p satisfying equation 6.41—remember that $\pi < 0$? Certainly not! Equation 6.41 is one equation in two variables λ and p, hence would be satisfied by infinitely many pairs of values of λ and p. Below we shall allow λ and p to vary with time and shall take a closer look at the scope for monetary policy.

Some Solutions Are Not Depending on λ and p

However this may be, we find g_P and g_w, and with them λ and p, to be absent from the growth-rate solutions for the eight variables *C, I, x, L, r, ϱ, S,* and *X* and from our solution for the level of the real rate of interest ϱ. Furthermore, subtract equation 6.30 from 6.34 and find the rate of growth of the real wage rate

$$g_{w/P} = g_w - g_P = g_a/\alpha \qquad (6.42)$$

from which λ and p have disappeared. Their disappearance has an important consequence now to be spelled out.

Friedman's Natural Rate of Unemployment

Friedman (1968: 8) defined a "natural" rate of unemployment as one at which "real wage rates are tending on the average to rise at a 'normal' secular rate, that is, at a rate that can be indefinitely maintained so long as capital formation, technological improvements, etc., remain on their long-run trends."[a] But our real wage rate was growing like that for any value of the employment fraction λ. Any value of the unemployment fraction $1 - \lambda$ was a Friedmanian natural rate! Friedman's natural rate was not unique.

Other Solutions Are Depending on λ and p

We find g_P or $g_{\bar{w}}$, and with them λ and p, to be present in the growth-rate solutions for the remaining five variables $D, M, P, w,$ and Y and in our solution for the level of the nominal rate of interest r. That brings us to the price-wage spiral.

The Price-Wage Spiral

Algebraic Solutions 6.30 and 6.34 Seen Graphically

Insert equation 6.28 and 6.35 into our price equation 6.5. Write the price and wage equations with g_w on the left-hand side:

---

[a] Friedman added another definition: "The 'natural rate of unemployment,' in other words, is the level that would be ground out by the Walrasian system of general equilibrium equations provided there is embedded in them the actual structural characteristics of the labor and commodity markets" Thus defined, is Friedman's natural rate unique?

Surveying the Phillips-curve literature, Santomero and Seater (1978: 515) found "a common albeit unverified assumption" that Walrasian general equilibrium is unique. Few macroeconomic writers offer general equilibria well enough specified to be shown to be unique!

Few of those who believe that labor markets will clear, demonstrate why. Those who do, usually apply search-theoretical explanations. As Tobin (1972: 6-9) points out, in such explanations all unemployment is voluntary. Do Walrasian equations, "provided there is embedded in them the actual structural characteristics of the labor and commodity markets," rule out involuntary unemployment? Friedman does not offer general equilibria well enough specified, let alone modified, to answer such a question.

$$g_w = g_a/\alpha + g_P \qquad\qquad (6.42)$$

$$g_w = p(1 - \lambda)^\pi + \Phi g_P \qquad\qquad (6.20)$$

and plot them in figure 6-1, having g_w on the vertical axis and g_P on the horizontal axis. The price equation 6.42 will then appear as a single straight line with the intercept g_a/α and the slope one. The wage equation 6.20 will appear as a family of straight lines with the intercepts $p(1 - \lambda)^\pi$ and the slope Φ. Our price-wage equilibrium 6.30 and 6.34 is represented graphically by the intersection between the price-equation line and a wage-equation line. Intersection points are marked by double circles in figure 6-1.

Sensitivity of the Price-Wage Equilibrium
to Φ and $p(1 - \lambda)^\pi$

Let Φ rise from zero to infinity and distinguish the five cases in figure 6-1.

First, let $\Phi = 0$. Failing to include labor's inflationary expectations, this is the case of the original Phillips curve. The wage equation appears as a family of horizontal lines drawn in the distance $p(1 - \lambda)^\pi$ from the horizontal axis. If $p(1 - \lambda)^\pi$ is less than, equal to, or greater than g_a/α then the rate of inflation g_P will be negative, zero, or positive, respectively. In other words, the rate of inflation is the higher the higher the employment fraction λ and the coefficient p.

Second, let $0 < \Phi < 1$. Now the wage equation appears as a family of positively sloped lines with the intercepts $p(1 - \lambda)^\pi$. Their slope Φ is less than one, hence they intersect the price-equation line from above, and the equilibria are stable. If, say, labor overshoots because it expects a g_P higher than the equilibrium value 6.30, entrepreneurs will respond along their price-equation line and raise price less than labor expected. Labor will go from there and respond along its wage-equation line and overshoot less. And so it goes. The parties are moving back toward the equilibrium point. Again if $p(1 - \lambda)^\pi$ is less than, equal to, or greater than g_a/α then the rate of inflation g_P will be negative, zero, or positive, respectively. Again the rate of inflation is the higher the higher the employment fraction λ and the coefficient p.

Third, let $\Phi \to 1$. Now the wage equation approaches a family of lines with unitary slope and the intercepts $p(1 - \lambda)^\pi$. All have the same slope as the price-equation line. If $p(1 - \lambda)^\pi$ is less than, equal to, or greater than g_a/α then there will be hyperdeflation with no equilibrium, infinitely many equilibria, or hyperinflation with no equilibrium, respectively: the limits of

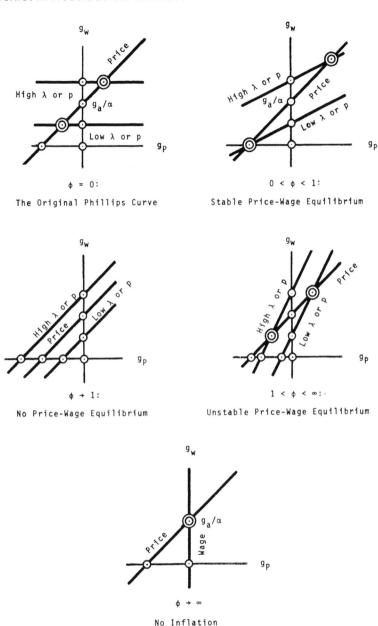

Figure 6-1. The Price–Wage Equilibrium: Five Possibilities

equation 6.30 and 6.34 are

$$\lim_{\Phi \to 1} g_P = \lim_{\Phi \to 1} g_w = \pm\infty$$

Fourth, let $1 < \Phi < \infty$. The wage equation appears as a family of positively sloped lines with the intercepts $p(1 - \lambda)^\pi$. But now their slope is greater than one, hence they intersect the price–equation line from below, and the equilibria are unstable. If, say, labor overshoots because it expects a g_P higher than the equilibrium value 6.30, entrepreneurs will respond along their price–equation line and raise price more than labor expected. Labor will go from there and respond along its wage–equation line and overshoot even more. And so it goes. The parties are now veering farther and farther away from the equilibrium point. Again the rate of inflation will depend on the employment fraction λ and the coefficient p but in an upside-down way. Now if $p(1 - \lambda)^\pi$ is less than, equal to, or greater than g_a/α then the rate of inflation g_P will be positive, zero, or negative, respectively. In other words, the rate of inflation is the *lower* the higher the employment fraction λ and the coefficient p!

Fifth, let $\Phi \to \infty$. Now the wage equation approaches a family of lines all of which are merging into the vertical axis. Divide the numerator and denominator of equation 6.34 by Φ and see that the limits of equations 6.30 and 6.34 are

$$\lim_{\Phi \to \infty} g_P = 0 \qquad \lim_{\Phi \to \infty} g_w = g_a/\alpha$$

Here an explosive situation might seem to have been defused into the harmless one of no inflation. But the equilibrium is still unstable.

A direct mapping of the function 6.30 would also have demonstrated the sensitivity of our price-wage equilibrium to Φ and $p(1 - \lambda)^\pi$. Such mapping is shown in figure 6–2.

Conclusion: Inflation Is an Empty Ritual

Subtracting equation 6.30 from 6.34 we found 6.42 according to which the rate of growth of the real wage rate was g_a/α. The employment fraction λ and the coefficient p had disappeared from 6.42, and figure 6–1 agrees: all our double–circled price-wage equilibria are located on the single price-equation line 6.42. With or without inflation labor can have a real wage rate growing at the rate g_a/α, no more, no less. In that sense inflation is an empty ritual. Why bother to go through with it? Could monetary policy gently persuade the parties not to bother? If so, what exactly should monetary policy be doing?

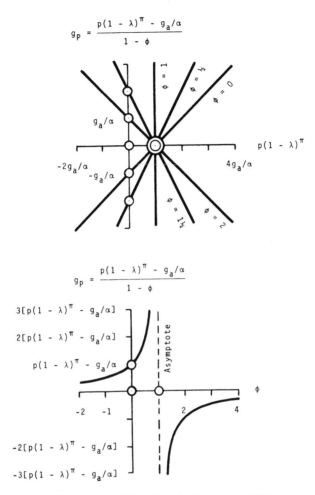

Figure 6-2. Mapping the Function 6.30

The Coefficient p as a Measure of the Inflationary
Potential and a Target for Monetary Policy

At given $0 < \Phi < 1$, our equilibrium solution 6.30 as well as figure 6-1 suggest that a lower rate of inflation g_P would require a depressed $p(1 - \lambda)^\pi$. That, in turn, would require either a depressed employment fraction λ or a depressed coefficient p. The monetary authorities, no doubt, would much prefer the latter to the former. A given reduction of inflation should be accomplished by depressing the employment fraction λ as little as possible.

The coefficient p is the weight with which unemployment $1 - \lambda$ makes itself felt in the Phillips function. If the monetary authorities could depress that weight, they would not have to depress λ itself.

In order to eliminate inflation, how far would p have to be depressed? The numerator of our equilibrium solution 6.30, and with it the rate of inflation g_P, could become zero in one and only one way, that is, if $p(1 - \lambda)^\pi = g_a/\alpha$ or

$$p = g_a/[\alpha(1 - \lambda)^\pi] \qquad (6.43)$$

shown as the double-circled point on the horizontal axis of figure 6-2. In the sense that inflation could be depressed to zero by depressing p to equation 6.43 the coefficient p may be called a measure of the inflationary potential of the economy—and may serve as a target for monetary policy.

It follows from 6.43 that the value to which p would have to be depressed to eliminate inflation is the higher the higher the technological progress g_a and the lower the employment fraction λ. In other words, high technological progress makes inflation fighting easier, but a high employment fraction makes it more difficult.

Monetary Policy

Our solutions 6.24 through 6.41 defined infinitely many steady-state equilibrium growth tracks. Once settled on any one of them, the economy will tend to stay on it: on such a track, whatever its employment fraction λ is and whatever its inflationary potential p is, expectations will be self-fulfilling, and self-fulfilling expectations are not abandoned easily. They will be abandoned only after new experience has proved them nonself-fulfilling.

Could such new experience be generated by monetary policy trying to switch the economy from one steady-state equilibrium growth track to another deemed more desirable? Let us at long last allow the employment fraction λ and the inflationary potential p to vary with time. Let us consider anti-inflation policy and employment policy separately.

Anti-inflation Policy: $0 < \Phi < 1$

As long as $0 < \Phi < 1$ a price-wage equilibrium exists and is stable. Let the monetary authorities try to switch the economy from a high-p steady-state equilibrium growth track to a low-p one. In their effort to depress p let them force the money supply to be growing at a rate lower than its steady-state equilibrium value 6.41. At so far unchanged expectations g_P, the nominal and real rates of interest will now rise above their equilibrium levels 6.40 and 6.39, respectively.

Write equation 6.15 as $S/X = \beta/\varrho$ and see that the desired capital coefficient is in inverse proportion to the real rate of interest. Consequently with the latter being above its equilibrium level 6.39 there is a once-and-for-all drop in the desired capital coefficient, and actual physical capital stock is suddenly in excess of the desired one. Desired physical investment is down for two reasons. First, for actual physical capital stock to be pared down to desired physical capital stock, physical investment will have to fall short of equation 6.16 for a while. Second, even after the paring down had been completed, 6.16 itself would be down: to make the smaller physical capital stock grow at the same rate would require a smaller physical investment.

According to equation 6.17 desired consumption is invariant with the real rate of interest. Raising the latter, then, will lower the right-hand side of the equilibrium condition 6.18: there will be negative excess demand.

The immediate effect is inventory accumulation, and inventory accumulation may release two responses: a price response and a quantity response. The hope underlying anti-inflation policy must be that the price response will dominate, that is, that inventory accumulation will be read as a signal to decelerate price. By depressing g_P such deceleration would depress the *second* term of the Phillips function 6.20. But as long as neither λ nor p had been affected, g_P would simply have been depressed below its equilibrium value 6.30. Expectations would no longer be self-fulfilling, and 6.30 would be trying to restore itself.

For anything of permanence to be accomplished, the *first* term of the Phillips function 6.20 must be depressed, by depressing either λ or p. Which of the two? Collective bargaining might hint that unless labor accepted a real wage rate growing at no more than its equilibrium rate g_a/α, inventory accumulation would be read as a signal to decelerate physical output and employment. Labor, in other words, might be coerced into following the price equation 6.42 rather than the wage equation 6.20. Labor, in still other words, might be coerced into depressing the first term of the Phillips function 6.20 by depressing the inflationary potential p rather than having the employment fraction λ depressed.

However this may be, decelerating price will not eliminate negative excess demand. According to equations 6.16 and 6.17 neither desired investment I nor desired consumption C will be stimulated, for price P appears nowhere in 6.16 and 6.17. Unable to eliminate negative excess demand, the falling inflationary potential p should keep falling. When it has fallen far enough to satisfy the policymaker, the latter may restore the real rate of interest to its equilibrium level 6.39. Only then will negative excess demand disappear.

Anti-inflation Policy: $\Phi \geq 1$

If $\Phi \geq 1$ a price-wage equilibrium is either unstable or nonexisting, respectively, and the price-wage spiral may accelerate as it did in 1967-1974. Recording the experience of seven OECD countries in 1959-1976, figure 6-3 provides a vivid illustration. Such wild price-wage spirals must be tamed, and the monetary authorities will tame them by refusing to meet the accelerating transaction demand for money. The effects of a refusal are much like those described for the case $\Phi < 1$. But the doses of monetary restraint might have to be heavier and to be applied incessantly.

Is $\Phi \geq 1$ likely to happen? Surveying 1963-1975 inflation theory Frisch (1977) reports that most empirical work has found $\Phi < 1$, that Gordon (1976) was unable to reject the hypothesis that $\Phi = 1$ after 1971, and that Φ may vary procyclically. The latter possibility fits the events recorded in figure 6-3.

Whether $\Phi < 1$ or $\Phi \geq 1$ the entire anti-inflation policy may be undone by the restoration of the real rate of interest to its equilibrium level 6.39, as we shall now see.

The Original Anti-inflation Effect Undone

Anti-inflation policy is an attempt to scale down the economy, that is, to switch it from a high-p steady-state equilibrium growth track to a low-p one. But more than scaling is involved when the real rate of interest is used as the instrument of such a policy. A bit of Austrian capital theory is involved as well: by writing equation 6.15 as $S/X = \beta/\varrho$, we saw that the desired capital coefficient is in inverse proportion to the real rate of interest. Consequently, just as the original raising of the real rate of interest above its equilibrium level 6.39 produced a once-and-for-all drop in the desired capital coefficient, a restoration to the equilibrium level 6.39 will produce a once-and-for-all jump exactly reversing the original drop. If the actual physical capital stock has been able to adjust downward to the original drop in the desired capital coefficient, it would now have to adjust upward again—undoing the original anti-inflation effect. Has it been able to?

It has. Through inventory accumulation under the persistent negative excess demand, actual physical capital stock has been able to adjust downward, and there is no clear physical boundary to inventory accumulation. Consequently, after the real rate of interest has been restored to its equilibrium level 6.39, actual physical capital stock will have to adjust upward again—undoing the original anti-inflation effect!

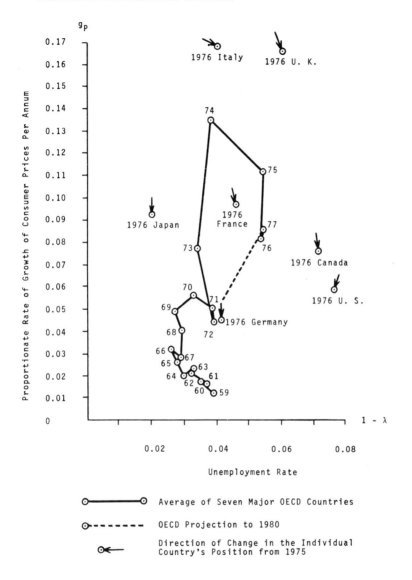

P. McCracken, G. Carli, H. Giersch, A. Karaosmanoglu, R. Komiya, A. Lindbeck, R. Marjolin, and R. Matthews, *Towards Full Employment and Price Stability, A Report to the OECD by a Group of Independent Experts*, OECD 1977, 314.

Figure 6-3. Inflation and Unemployment, Seven OECD Countries, 1959–1976

Employment Policy

Suppose it is not considered enough to reduce inflation without reducing the employment fraction λ. The latter should be *raised*. Let the monetary authorities try to switch the economy from a low-λ steady-state equilibrium growth track to a high-λ one. In their effort to raise λ let them allow the money supply to be growing at a rate higher than its steady-state equilibrium value 6.41. At so far unchanged expectations g_P, the nominal and real rates of interest will now fall below their equilibrium levels 6.40 and 6.39, respectively.

We wrote equation 6.15 as $S/X = \beta/\varrho$ and saw that the desired capital coefficient is in inverse proportion to the real rate of interest. Consequently with the latter being below its equilibrium level 6.39 there is a once-and-for-all jump in the desired capital coefficient, and actual physical capital stock is suddenly falling short of the desired one. Desired physical investment is up for two reasons. First, for actual physical capital stock to catch up with desired physical capital stock, physical investment will have to exceed equation 6.16 for a while. Second, even after the catching up had been completed, 6.16 itself would be up: to make the larger physical capital stock grow at the same rate would require a larger physical investment.

According to equation 6.17 desired consumption is invariant with the real rate of interest. Lowering the latter, then, will raise the right-hand side of the equilibrium condition 6.18: there will be positive excess demand.

The immediate effect is inventory depletion, and inventory depletion may release two responses: a price response and a quantity response. The hope underlying employment policy must be that the quantity response will dominate, that is, that inventory depletion will be read as a signal to accelerate physical output. Can entrepreneurs heed the signal? Write equation 6.4 as $L = \alpha PX/w$. So accelerating physical output X would accelerate employment L and raise the employment fraction λ, always feasible under unemployment.

Accelerating physical output will not eliminate positive excess demand. According to equations 6.16 and 6.17 both desired investment I and desired consumption C are in direct proportion to physical output X. Consequently the difference $C + I - X$, positive excess demand, will also be in direct proportion to physical output X. Unable to eliminate positive excess demand, the expanding employment fraction λ should keep expanding. When it has expanded far enough to satisfy the policymaker, the latter may restore the real rate of interest to its equilibrium level 6.39. Only then will positive excess demand disappear.

May the entire employment policy be undone by the restoration of the real rate of interest to its equilibrium level 6.39—the way anti-inflation policy was?

The Original Employment Effect Not Undone

Employment policy is an attempt to scale up the economy, that is, to switch it from a low-λ steady-state equilibrium growth track to a high-λ one. But again more than scaling is involved when the real rate of interest is used as the instrument of such a policy. Again a bit of Austrian capital theory is involved, too: by writing equation 6.15 as $S/X = \beta/\varrho$ we saw that the desired capital coefficient is in inverse proportion to the real rate of interest. Consequently, just as the original lowering of the real rate of interest below its equilibrium level 6.39 produced a once-and-for-all jump in the desired capital coefficient, a restoration to the equilibrium level 6.39 will produce a once-and-for-all drop exactly reversing the original jump. If the actual physical capital stock has been able to adjust upward to the original jump in the desired capital coefficient, it would now have to adjust downward again—undoing the original employment effect. Has it been able to?

It has not. Through inventory depletion under the persistent positive excess demand, actual physical capital stock has been able to adjust upward a bit, but there is a clear physical boundary to inventory depletion. Once all inventory is gone there is no way of satisfying all demand. If an individual entrepreneur has succeeded in raising his capital coefficient, he must have done so at the expense of others. Consequently, after the restoration of the equilibrium level 6.39 of the real rate of interest, actual physical capital stock will hardly have to adjust downward. There is no undoing of the original employment effect!

Comparison

The dilemma of monetary policy is neatly illustrated by the fact that anti-inflation policy and employment policy are based on mutually exclusive hopes. The former hopes for a price response, the latter for a quantity response. The actions taken by the monetary authorities under the two policies are mutually exclusive: one policy is the other in reverse.

But between the two policies there is a distinct asymmetry ignored by Keynesians and monetarists alike. Once the policy interference with equilibrium is terminated and the real rate of interest is restored to its equilibrium level 6.39, such restoration may undo the original effect of an anti-inflation policy but not that of an employment policy. In this sense the latter is more likely to succeed than the former. The asymmetry is the result of a bit of Austrian capital theory inherent in a neoclassical growth model but absent from Keynesian and monetarist models alike.

How Far Did Our Synthesis Go?

We opened the neoclassical growth model to unemployment and inflation and solved for its steady-state equilibrium rates of growth and interest. To what extent could Wicksellian, Keynesian, monetarist, and neoclassical ideas coexist in it?

Wicksell

Was our model Wicksellian? Yes, in the sense that in it money mattered but mattered only via its effect upon the rate of interest. And yes in the sense that our model determined a rate of interest at which saving equals investment. But that equality guaranteed neither full employment nor absence of inflation. Whatever the values of their employment fraction λ and their inflationary potential p, our infinitely many solutions all satisfy equation 6.37 that saving equals investment.

Keynes

To J.B. Say output was bounded by supply. Demand was no problem: supply would generate its own demand. To J.M. Keynes output was bounded by demand. Supply was no problem: demand would generate its own supply. Output would be controllable to the extent demand was. Was our model Keynesian? Yes, in the sense that output was bounded by demand and touched no supply bound: $0 < \lambda < 1$. Was demand controllable? Certainly. The monetary authorities could expand their stock of claims, and with it the money supply, more or less rapidly. The pace at which they would expand it would affect the yield of the claims and might generate positive or negative excess demand, respectively. But whether the response to such excess demand would be a price response or a quantity response was beyond the control of the monetary authorities. Furthermore, restoration of equilibrium would undo the original effect of an anti-inflation policy but not that of an employment policy. Such asymmetry was the result of Austrian capital theory absent from Keynesian models.

Monetarists

Was our model monetarist? Yes, but only in the sense that it might generate inflation and that it distinguished between a nominal and a real rate of interest. In its infinitely many solutions, one for each value of the employment fraction λ, the real wage rate was found to be growing at the same rate, and in that sense any value of the unemployment fraction $1 - \lambda$ was a Friedmanian "natural" rate of unemployment. Friedman's natural rate of unemployment was not unique. Further doubt on monetarist doctrine was cast by our asymmetry between anti-inflation policy and employment policy. Restoration of equilibrium would undo the original effect of an anti-inflation policy but not that of an employment policy. Such asymmetry was the result of Austrian capital theory equally absent from Keynesian and monetarist models.

Neoclassicals

Was our model neoclassical? Yes, in the sense that it simulated labor-capital substitution in a steady-state equilibrium growth setting and had an Austrian capital theory built into it according to which the desired capital coefficient was in inverse proportion to the real rate of interest. But in one respect our model was not neoclassical: its goods and money markets cleared in equilibrium, but its labor market did not. The model had room for involuntary unemployment: $0 < \lambda < 1$. It had infinitely many solutions, offering scope for controlling demand.

References

O. Eckstein and J.A. Girola, "Long-Term Properties of the Price-Wage Mechanism in the United States, 1891 to 1977," *Rev. Econ. Statist.,* Aug. 1978 *60,* 323-333.

I. Fisher, "Appreciation and Interest," *Publications of the American Economic Association,* Aug. 1896, *11,* 331-442.

——, *The Theory of Interest,* New York 1930.

M. Friedman, "The Role of Monetary Policy," *Amer. Econ. Rev.,* Mar. 1968, *58,* 1-17.

H. Frisch, "Inflation Theory 1963-1975: A 'Second Generation' Survey," *J. Econ. Lit.,* Dec. 1977, *15,* 1289-1317.

R.J. Gordon, "Recent Developments in the Theory of Inflation and Unemployment," *J. Monetary Econ.,* Apr. 1976, *2,* 185-219.

R.F. Harrod, *Towards a Dynamic Economics,* London 1948.

J.M. Keynes, *A Treatise on Money, I,* London 1930.

——, *The General Theory of Employment, Interest and Money,* London 1936.

P. McCracken, G. Carli, H. Giersch, A. Karaosmanoglu, R. Komiya, A. Lindbeck, R. Marjolin, and R. Matthews, *Towards Full Employ-*

ment and Price Stability, A Report to the OECD by a Group of Independent Experts, OECD 1977.

R.A. Mundell, *Monetary Theory: Inflation, Interest, and Growth in the World Economy,* Pacific Palisades 1971.

A.W. Phillips, "The Relation between Unemployment and the Rate of Change of Money Wage Rates in the United Kingdom, 1861-1957." *Economica,* Nov. 1958, *25,* 283-299.

A.M. Santomero and J.J. Seater, "The Inflation–Unemployment Trade-Off: A Critique of the Literature," *J. Econ. Lit.,* June 1978, *16,* 499-544.

R.M. Solow, "A Contribution to the Theory of Economic Growth," *Quart. J. Econ.,* Feb. 1956, *70,* 65-94.

J. Tobin, "Inflation and Unemployment," *Amer. Econ. Rev.,* Mar. 1972, *62,* 1-18.

A.R.J. Turgot, "Réflexions sur la formation et la distribution des richesses," *Ephémérides du citoyen,* Nov. 1769-Jan. 1770. *Reflections on the Formation and the Distribution of Riches,* New York 1898.

K. Wicksell, *Föreläsningar i nationalekonomi, II,* Lund 1906. *Lectures on Political Economy, II,* London 1935.

7

A Corporate Economy: Inflation, Bonds, and Shares

Until now all saving was presumably personal saving, and its placement was presumbably interest-bearing. Bonds, shares, and the undistributed profits of the corporations issuing them were never mentioned.

The purpose of this chapter is to introduce corporate finance in our steady-state growth and inflation model. We shall assume stationary fractions of investment financed by bond and share issues. Given those fractions we shall then determine the fractions, also stationary, of profits absorbed by the interest and dividend bills. The algebraic relationship between the two pairs of fractions will turn out to be simple and very sensitive to the rate of inflation.

Our simple algebraic relationship reveals a fundamental difference between bond and share financing. Its pratical consequence is that inflation will tilt the debt-equity balance in favor of debt.

Notation

Let us expand the notation of chapter 6 by the following eight variables:

$\delta \equiv$ dividend payment per annum per share
$H \equiv$ a stationary proportionality factor
$h \equiv$ a stationary proportionality factor
$i \equiv$ interest payment per annum per bond
$k \equiv$ present gross worth of a security
$n \equiv$ present net worth of a security
$\Pi \equiv$ price of a security
$Q \equiv$ physical quantity of a security in existence

The Model

The equations of chapter 6 will be referred to, four of them so often that we repeat them here: define the proportionate rate of growth

$$g_v \equiv \frac{dv}{dt} \frac{1}{v} \tag{7.1}$$

Define investment as the derivative of capital stock with respect to time:

$$I \equiv \frac{dS}{dt} \qquad (7.2)$$

Physical marginal productivity of capital stock is

$$\varkappa \equiv \frac{\partial X}{\partial S} = \beta \frac{X}{S} \qquad (7.3)$$

Multiply by value of capital stock PS and define profits before interest and dividends as

$$Z \equiv \varkappa PS \qquad (7.4)$$

Let all firms be corporations financing their investment from three sources. First, a corporation may issue immortal bonds, sell them to savers, personal and corporate, and pay interest on them forever after. Second, a corporation may issue immortal shares, sell them to savers, personal and corporate, and pay dividends on them forever. Not all profits need be distributed as interest and dividends. The undistributed profits of one corporation may either be placed in bonds and shares issued by other corporations and if so, have already been allowed for by our first two sources. Or, third, the undistributed profits may be placed in the purchase of physical assets by the corporation itself. If so, the fractions of investment financed by issuing bonds and shares will add up to less than one.

Before studying those fractions let us briefly examine bond and share prices.

Bond and Share Prices as Capitalizations of Future Cash Flows

Irving Fisher (1907; 1930) insisted that the present worth of a financial asset would depend solely on the sum of the discounted future cash flows paid to its owner. To our bonds and shares let us apply Fisher's principle, so strongly endorsed by Lintner (1962: 268; 1975: 260), who called Fisher at once the Adam Smith and the Léon Walras of finance.

The Price of a Bond as Capitalized Interest

At time t let an immortal bond be paying the interest $i(t)$ dollars per annum. As seen from present time τ, the interest payment $i(t)$ is worth

$i(t)e^{-r(t-\tau)}$, where r is our stationary nominal rate of interest used as a discount rate. Define present gross worth of the bond as the present worth of all its future interest payments over its entire life

$$k_b(\tau) \equiv \int_\tau^\infty i(t)e^{-r(t-\tau)}\,dt \qquad (7.5)$$

The interest payment is stationary:

$$i(t) = i(\tau) \qquad (7.6)$$

Insert equation 7.6 into 7.5 and write the latter:

$$k_b(\tau) = \int_\tau^\infty i(\tau)e^{-r(t-\tau)}\,dt$$

Here $i(\tau)$ is not a function of t, hence may be taken outside the integral sign. Our r was said to be stationary, hence the coefficient r of t is stationary. Assume $r > 0$ and find the integral to be

$$k_b = i/r \qquad (7.7)$$

Find present net worth of the bond as its gross worth *minus* its price:

$$n_b \equiv k_b - \Pi_b = i/r - \Pi_b$$

Since equation 7.6 is virtually certain, the net worth will be common to virtually all bondholders. If $\Pi_b > i/r$ net worth will be negative, and virtually all bondholders would be induced to sell bonds. The scramble to do so will bring price down. If

$$\Pi_b = i/r \qquad (7.8)$$

net worth will be zero, and bondholders would be induced to neither buy nor sell. If $\Pi_b < i/r$ net worth will be positive, and virtually all bondholders would be induced to buy bonds. The scramble to do so will bring price up. At any time, then, the overwhelmingly likely price of bonds is equation 7.8.

Our steady-state growth and inflation model displayed a stationary nominal rate of interest r; compare our solution 6.31. Differentiating equation 7.8 with respect to time we find, therefore, the rate of growth of Π_b to be the same as that of the interest payment i. But according to equation 7.6 the interest payment i was stationary. Consequently

$$g_{\Pi b} = g_i = 0 \qquad (7.9)$$

The price 7.8 of a bond is a capitalization of its current interest payment i. The capitalization factor is $1/r$ or the reciprocal of the nominal rate of interest. But we may just as well write equation 7.8 as

$$r = i/\Pi_b \tag{7.10}$$

or, in English, our nominal rate of interest may be practically represented by the bond yield.

The Price of a Share as Capitalized Dividends

At time t let an immortal share be paying the dividend $\delta(t)$ dollars per annum. As seen from present time τ, the dividend payment $\delta(t)$ is worth $\delta(t)e^{-r(t-\tau)}$, where again r is the stationary nominal rate of interest used as a discount rate. Define present gross worth of the share as the present worth of all its future dividend payments over its entire life

$$k_s(\tau) \equiv \int_\tau^\infty \delta(t)e^{-r(t-\tau)}dt \tag{7.11}$$

Let the shareholder expect the dividend payment to be growing at the stationary rate g_δ:

$$\delta(t) = \delta(\tau)e^{g_\delta(t-\tau)} \tag{7.12}$$

Insert equation 7.12 into 7.11 and write the latter as

$$k_s(\tau) = \int_\tau^\infty \delta(\tau)e^{-(r-g_\delta)(t-\tau)}dt$$

Here $\delta(\tau)$ is not a function of t, hence may be taken outside the integral sign. Our g_δ and r were both said to be stationary, hence the coefficient $(r - g_\delta)$ of t is stationary. Assume $r - g_\delta > 0$ and find the integral to be

$$k_s = \delta/(r - g_\delta) \tag{7.13}$$

Find present net worth of the share as its gross worth *minus* its price:

$$n_s \equiv k_s - \Pi_s = \delta/(r - g_\delta) - \Pi_s$$

Let most shareholders have the expectation 7.12, then the net worth will be common to most shareholders. If $\Pi_s > \delta/(r - g_\delta)$ net worth will be negative, and most shareholders would be induced to sell shares. The scramble to do so will bring price down. If

$$\Pi_s = \delta/(r - g_\delta) \qquad (7.14)$$

net worth will be zero, and most shareholders would be induced to neither buy nor sell. If $\Pi_s < \delta/(r - g_\delta)$ net worth will be positive, and most shareholders would be induced to buy shares. The scramble to do so will bring price up. At any time, then, the most likely price of shares is equation 7.14.

Our steady-state growth and inflation model displayed a stationary nominal rate of interest r; compare our solution 6.31. The rate of growth g_δ of the dividend payment was stationary, too. Differentiating equation 7.14 with respect to time we find, therefore, the rate of growth of Π_s to be the same as that of the dividend payment δ:

$$g_{\Pi s} = g_\delta \qquad (7.15)$$

Equation 7.24 below will assume share prices and goods prices to be growing at the same rate: $g_{\Pi s} = g_P$. If so, the difference $r - g_\delta$ becomes $r - g_P$, which is the real rate of interest; compare equation 6.38. We may then write equation 7.14 as

$$\Pi_s = \delta/\varrho \qquad (7.16)$$

The price 7.16 of a share is a capitalization of its current dividend payment δ. The capitalization factor is $1/\varrho$ or the reciprocal of the real rate of interest. But we may just as well write equation 7.16 as

$$\varrho = \delta/\Pi_s \qquad (7.17)$$

or, in English, our real rate of interest may be practically represented by the dividend yield.

Equations 7.10 and 7.17 saying that the bond and dividend yields are practical representatives of the nominal and real rates of interest, respectively, are testable propositions, and appendix 7A will test them.

The Fractions of Investment Financed by Bond and Share Issues

Bond Issues

All bonds being immortal, the physical quantity of new bonds issued is the time derivative of the physical quantity of bonds in existence. Use definition

7.1 and let that time derivative be in proportion to the *money value* of investment:

$$\frac{dQ_b}{dt} \equiv g_{Qb} Q_b = h_b IP \tag{7.18}$$

where the proportionality factor h_b is a stationary variable.

The dollar proceeds of a new bond issue is physical quantity of new bonds issued *times* price of a bond:

$$g_{Qb} \Pi_b Q_b = H_b IP \tag{7.19}$$

where H_b is a new variable defined as

$$H_b \equiv h_b \Pi_b \tag{7.20}$$

and where $0 \le H_b < 1$. (H_b cannot be one: corporations without shares would not be corporations!) According to equation 7.9 the price of bonds Π_b was stationary. Consequently the dollar proceeds of the new bond issue will finance a stationary fraction H_b of the money value of investment.

Share Issues

All shares being immortal, the physical quantity of new shares issued is the time derivative of the physical quantity of shares in existence. Use definition 7.1 and let that time derivative be in proportion to *physical* investment:

$$\frac{dQ_s}{dt} \equiv g_{Qs} Q_s = h_s I \tag{7.21}$$

where the proportionality factor h_s is a stationary variable.

The dollar proceeds of a new share issue is physical quantity of new shares issued *times* price of a share:

$$g_{Qs} \Pi_s Q_s = H_s IP \tag{7.22}$$

where H_s is a new variable defined as

$$H_s \equiv h_s \Pi_s / P \tag{7.23}$$

and where $0 < H_s \le 1$. (H_s cannot be zero: corporations without shares would not be corporations!) Our new variable H_s would be stationary if share prices and goods prices were growing at the same rate:

$$g_{\Pi s} = g_P \tag{7.24}$$

Let equation 7.24 be satisfied. Then the dollar proceeds of a new share issue will finance a stationary fraction H_s of the money value of investment. Equation 7.24 is a testable proposition, and appendix 7B will test it.

The Fractions of Profits Absorbed by Interest and Dividends

Interest Payment per Bond

Regardless of their date of issue let all bonds carry the same face value and the same face interest rate. Then at any time all bonds are entitled to the same dollar amount of interest i per annum. Use equation 7.8 to write that amount as

$$i = \Pi_b r \tag{7.25}$$

Physical Quantity of Bonds in Existence

The physical quantity of bonds in existence at time τ is the accumulated physical quantity of bonds issued over the entire past. Use equation 7.18 to write this as

$$Q_b(\tau) \equiv \int_{-\infty}^{\tau} \frac{dQ_b(t)}{dt}\, dt = \int_{-\infty}^{\tau} h_b I(t) P(t)\, dt \tag{7.26}$$

Solutions 6.26 and 6.30 found I and P to be growing at the stationary rates g_X and g_P, respectively:

$$I(t) = I(\tau) e^{-g_X(\tau - t)} \tag{7.27}$$

$$P(t) = P(\tau) e^{-g_P(\tau - t)} \tag{7.28}$$

Insert equations 7.27 and 7.28 into the integral 7.26 and write the latter as

$$Q_b(\tau) = \int_{-\infty}^{\tau} h_b I(\tau) P(\tau) e^{-(g_P + g_X)(\tau - t)}\, dt \tag{7.29}$$

Neither h_b, $P(\tau)$, nor $I(\tau)$ is a function of t, hence may be taken outside the integral sign. Our g_P and g_X were both said to be stationary, hence the coefficient $(g_P + g_X)$ of t is stationary. Assume $g_P + g_X > 0$. As a result, find the integral to be

$$Q_b = h_b IP/(g_P + g_X) \qquad (7.30)$$

Since h_b, g_P, and g_X are stationary, the rate of growth of Q_b is

$$g_{Qb} = g_P + g_X \qquad (7.31)$$

Interest Bill

The interest bill is interest payment per bond *times* physical quantity of bonds in existence. So multiply equations 7.25 and 7.30, use the definition 7.20 of H_b, and write the interest bill as

$$iQ_b = H_b IPr/(g_P + g_X) \qquad (7.32)$$

Dividend Payment per Share

Regardless of their date of issue let all shares carry the same rights. Then at a particular time all shares are entitled to the same dollar amount of dividends δ per annum. Use equation 7.16 to write that amount as

$$\delta = \Pi_s \varrho \qquad (7.33)$$

Physical Quantity of Shares in Existence

The physical quantity of shares in existence at time τ is the accumulated physical quantity of shares issued over the entire past. Use equation 7.21 to write this as

$$Q_s(\tau) \equiv \int_{-\infty}^{\tau} \frac{dQ_s(t)}{dt} dt = \int_{-\infty}^{\tau} h_s I(t) dt \qquad (7.34)$$

Solution 6.26 found I to be growing at the stationary rate g_X:

$$I(t) = I(\tau) e^{-g_X(\tau - t)} \qquad (7.35)$$

Insert equation 7.35 into the integral 7.34 and write the latter as

$$Q_s(\tau) = \int_{-\infty}^{\tau} h_s I(\tau) e^{-g_X(\tau - t)} dt \qquad (7.36)$$

Neither h_s nor $I(\tau)$ is a function of t, hence may be taken outside the integral sign. Our g_X was said to be stationary, hence the coefficient g_X of t is stationary. Assume $g_X > 0$. As a result, find the integral to be

$$Q_s = h_s I/g_X \qquad (7.37)$$

Since h_s and g_X are stationary, the rate of growth of Q_s is

$$g_{Qs} = g_X \qquad (7.38)$$

Dividend Bill

The dividend bill is dividend payment per share *times* physical quantity of shares in existence. So multiply equations 7.33 and 7.37, use the definition 7.23 of H_s, and write the dividend bill as

$$\delta Q_s = H_s IP\varrho/g_X \qquad (7.39)$$

The Interest and Dividend Fractions of Profits

The interest fraction of profits will be iQ_b/Z. Insert expression 7.32 for the interest bill, insert our definition 7.4 of the profits bill, and recall that according to our definitions 7.1 and 7.2 $S \equiv I/g_S$; according to equation 6.14 $\varkappa = \varrho$; 6.33 $g_S = g_X$; 6.38 $r = \varrho + g_P$. We may then write the interest fraction of profits as

$$iQ_b/Z = \Psi H_b \qquad \text{where} \qquad (7.40)$$

$$\Psi \equiv (1 + g_P/\varrho)/(1 + g_P/g_X) \qquad (7.41)$$

The dividend fraction of profits will be $\delta Q_s/Z$. Insert expression 7.39 for the dividend bill and again insert equations 7.4, 7.1, 7.2, 6.14, and 6.33. We may then write the dividend fraction of profits as

$$\delta Q_s/Z = H_s \qquad (7.42)$$

In summary, the interest fraction of profits is *not* equal to the bond fraction H_b of investment but equal to ΨH_b. By contrast, the dividend fraction of profits *is* equal to the share fraction H_s of investment. The practical importance of this difference must depend upon the value of Ψ. As defined by equation 7.41, Ψ is a function of the rate of inflation g_P. Let us examine that function.

The Ratio Ψ as a Function of the
Rate of Inflation g_P

In the absence of inflation $g_P = 0$ and $\Psi = 1$. In the presence of inflation $g_P > 0$, and it will matter which is greater, ϱ or g_X. According to equation 6.39, $\varrho = \beta g_X/(1 - c)$, and in the United States $\beta > 1 - c$. Consequently $\varrho > g_X$ and $\Psi < 1$. In that case, how precisely does Ψ depend upon the rate of inflation g_P? Divide the numerator and the denominator of Ψ by g_P and find two limits of equation 7.41:

$$\lim_{g_P \to -g_X} \frac{1/g_P + 1/\varrho}{1/g_P + 1/g_X} = \infty \qquad (7.43)$$

$$\lim_{g_P \to \infty} \frac{1/g_P + 1/\varrho}{1/g_P + 1/g_X} = g_X/\varrho \qquad (7.44)$$

Consequently the function has a vertical asymptote for $g_P = -g_X$ and a horizontal one for g_P rising without bounds. Figure 7–1 shows[a] the function for $g_X/\varrho = 9/20$.

The steep decline of the function Ψ as g_P rises ever so slightly above zero shows that our difference between bond and share financing is practically important already at low rates of inflation: at merely 3 percent inflation Ψ has already declined to 0.73.

Is there an intuitive explanation for such a powerful effect?

A Simple Example

Consider a steady-state rate of inflation of 0.06 per annum. The price of goods is then doubling every twelve years. Let the nominal and real rates of interest equal 0.12 and 0.06 per annum, respectively.

Let a dollar's worth of capital be raised by issuing a bond. At the time of issue, according to equation 7.10, the bond selling at one dollar must be carrying an interest payment of $i =$ twelve cents per annum at that time. The interest payment on the bond is stationary; consequently the cost of having raised that dollar remains twelve cents per annum forever.

By contrast, let a dollar's worth of capital be raised by issuing a share. At the time of issue, according to equation 7.17, the share selling at one dollar must be carrying a dividend payment of $\delta =$ six cents per annum at that time. But the dividend payment on the share is growing at 6 percent per

---

[a] Why show it for $g_X/\varrho = 9/20$? According to equation 6.39, $g_X/\varrho = (1 - c)/\beta$. In the United States, capital consumption allowances are roughly one-half of gross investment, and gross investment is roughly 16 percent of gross output. Consequently net investment is roughly 9 percent of net output, and $1 - c = 0.09$. As shown in chapter 4, β is roughly 0.20.

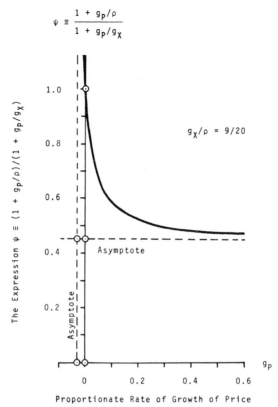

Figure 7-1 The Ratio between the Interest Fraction of Profits and the Bond
Fraction of Investment at a Varying Inflation Rate

annum. As a result, on a dollar raised now, twelve years hence twelve cents
and twenty-four years hence twenty-four cents will be paid.

Why would anyone buy a dollar's worth of bonds which, twenty-four
years hence, will yield twelve cents per annum when he could have bought a
dollar's worth of shares which, twenty-four years hence, would have
yielded twenty-four cents per annum? If he does, isn't he somehow being
cheated?

In the rarefied air of our steady-state inflation model the nominal rate
of interest is always fully adjusted to a perfectly foreseen rate of inflation.
Looking forward, our security buyers know what they are doing. They are
paying the prices 7.8 and 7.14 representing what bonds and shares, respectively, are worth to them, given the discount rate r. Equation 6.38 still holds
and suggests a simple way in which bondholders may and will keep the real
value of their aggregate interest-bearing assets intact: with the difference g_P
between the nominal and real rates of interest they may and will purchase
more bonds. The physical quantity of bonds is growing more rapidly than

that of shares. According to equations 7.31 and 7.38 the rates of growth are $g_P + g_X$ and g_X, respectively. At the stationary price Π_b of bonds, that will prevent any erosion of the real value of the aggregate physical quantity of bonds. In this sense nobody is being cheated.

Conclusion

We have introduced corporations in our steady–state growth and inflation model. We have found that if, under inflation, a corporation finances the fraction H_b of its investment by issuing bonds, the interest on them will absorb annually a fraction of profits less than H_b. But if the corporation finances the fraction H_s of its investment by issuing shares, the dividends on them will absorb annually a fraction of profits equal to H_s.

In this sense inflation tilts the debt–equity balance in favor of debt—the more so the higher the rate of steady–state inflation. Our finding is nontrivial: it included an assumption that the nominal rate of interest was always fully adjusted to a perfectly foreseen rate of steady–state inflation.

Appendix 7A: Testing the Goodness of the Bond Yield and the Dividend Yield as Representatives of the Nominal and Real Rates of Interest, Respectively

Let us observe the United States and the Federal Republic of Germany over the fifteen inflationary years 1963–1977. Let the bond yield in the United States be the yield of Moody's corporate Baa bonds, in Germany the yield of all industrial bonds. Let the dividend yield in the United States be a Standard & Poor common stock yield, in Germany the yield of all corporate stock. Figure 7–2 plots the bond yield *minus* the dividend yield as a function of the rate of inflation. If the bond yield and the dividend yield were perfect representatives of the nominal and real rates of interest, respectively, their difference would always equal the rate of inflation, and all observations would lie on the 45° lines of figure 7–2. Do they?

Not quite. In the United States the years 1971 and 1972 and in Germany the years 1967–1969 are lying far above the 45° lines. In both countries those were years of subsiding inflation—in the United States the reason was wage and price controls; in Germany the reason was a mild recession. In both countries the security markets apparently considered the news to be too good to last.

In the United States, but not in Germany, the oil crisis years 1974 and 1975 are lying far below the 45° line. Here the security markets apparently considered the two–digit–inflation news too bad to last.

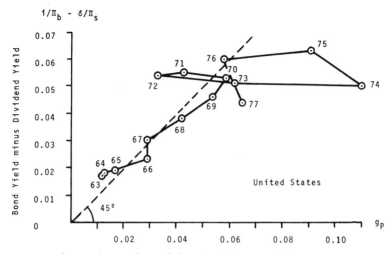

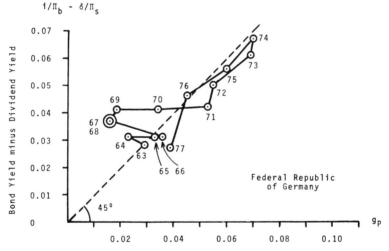

Economic Report of the President Transmitted to the Congress January 1978,
Washington, D. C., 1978, 318, 332, and 360.

Monatsberichte der Deutschen Bundesbank 23, Oct. 1971, 51*.

Monatsberichte der Deutschen Bundesbank 30, May 1978, 53* and 68*.

Figure 7-2. Testing the Goodness of the Bond Yield and the Dividend
Yield as Representatives of the Nominal and Real Rates of In-
terest, Respectively, United States and Federal Republic of
Germany, 1963–1977

Real-world inflation is neither steady-state nor perfectly foreseen. Even so, the bond yield and the dividend yield do seem to represent tolerably well the nominal and real rates of interest, respectively.

Appendix 7B: Goods Prices and Share Prices

On semilogarithmic scales figures 7-3 through 7-5 show goods price and share price indices as functions of time. Such a scale permits easy comparisons between index series whose base years differ or are occasionally changing. We observe the United States 1907-1977, the German Reich 1904-1943, and the Federal Republic of Germany 1953-1974. If the price of goods and the price of shares were always growing at the same rate, the index curves in figures 7-3 through 7-5 would always be parallel. Are they?

In both countries the swings of both goods and share prices are rather long ones, so the answer will depend upon the period considered. Consider a U.S. shareholder buying shares in 1910. In 1977 his shares would be worth 10.5 times as much, while the consumer price index would be merely 6.3 times as high. Had he waited until the summer of 1929 and had he been able to hold on to his shares, they would have risen 3.8 times by 1977 while the consumer price index would have risen 3.5 times. The worst the shareholder could have done was to buy shares around 1965.

The vagaries of U.S. share prices have their counterparts in Germany, but with the effects of two military defeats and hyperinflation superimposed upon them. Shares were not particularly attractive the last ten years before World War I. But both the first stabilization of the mark, in 1924, and the second one, in 1948, would have been excellent times to buy shares.

Cut off from doing controlled experiments of his own, an economist must watch with intense interest the extremes arranged by the economy itself. In such extremes he may find major forces overwhelming random variations. One such extreme was the 1922-1923 German hyperinflation. It will need a diagram all to itself, that is, figure 7-5, using a very small logarithmic unit of measurement on its vertical axis. That way the axis can go all the way from 10 to 10^{14}, thus capturing the trillions of hyperinflation. Figure 7-5 shows how well the share prices followed the consumer prices into the trillions!

Real-world inflation is neither steady-state nor perfectly foreseen. Even so, in the long run share prices do follow goods prices tolerably well.

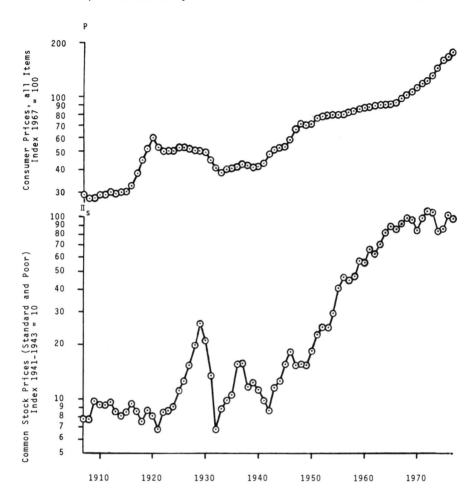

U. S. Department of Commerce, Bureau of the Census, *Long Term Economic Growth 1860 1970*, Washington, D. C., 1973, 222-225.

Economic Report of the President Transmitted to the Congress January 1978, **Washington**, D. C., 1978, 313 and 360.

Figure 7-3. Consumer and Common Stock Prices, United States, 1907–
1977

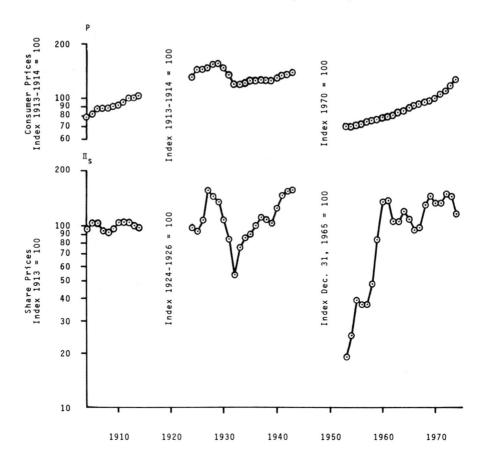

Deutsche Bundesbank, *Deutsches Geld- und Bankwesen in Zahlen 1876-1975*, Frankfurt am Main 1976, 3, 5, 6, and 7.

Figure 7-4. Consumer Prices and Share Prices, Germany, 1904–1914 and 1924–1943, and Federal Republic of Germany, 1953–1974

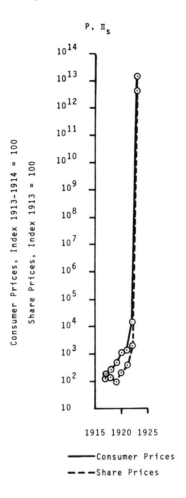

Figure 7-5. Consumer Prices and Share Prices in Hyperinflation, Germany, 1917–1923

References

Deutsche Bundesbank, *Deutsches Geld- und Bankwesen in Zahlen 1876–1975,* Frankfurt am Main, 1976, 3, 5, 6, and 7.

———, *Monatsberichte der Deutschen Bundesbank 23,* Oct. 1971, 51*.

———, *Monatsberichte der Deutschen Bundesbank 30,* May 1978, 53* and 68*.

I. Fisher, *The Rate of Interest,* New York 1907.

———, *The Theory of Interest,* New York 1930.

J. Lintner, "Dividends, Earnings, Leverage, Stock Prices and the Supply of Capital to Corporations," *Rev. Econ. Statist.,* Aug. 1962, *44,* 243–269.

———, "Inflation and Security Returns," *J. Finance,* May 1975, *30,* 259–280.

U.S. Government, Department of Commerce, Bureau of the Census, *Long Term Economic Growth 1860–1970,* Washington, D.C., 1973, 222–225.

———, *Economic Report of the President Transmitted to the Congress January 1978,* Washington, D.C., 1978, 313 and 360.

8

Mortal Capital Stock: Gross and Net Investment

Until now capital stock was assumed to be immortal. No replacement was ever necessary; all output was net output, and all investment net investment.

Should we apologize for such a narrow approach? By ignoring replacement are we losing sight of something important? Denison (1974: 9) would answer no: "Gross national product, as its name implies, is a partially duplicated measure of production, which therefore is not suitable for growth analysis." The output whose maximization may be the objective of policy, Denison adds, is net not gross output. One would wish to maximize capital consumption incurred in the production of television sets no more than one would wish to maximize the metal absorbed in their production.

While not apologizing for our narrow approach we might still be curious to see what was left out of sight. What difference, if any, would it make to growth rates, investment, and interest rates if capital stock were mortal? Let us expand the notation of chapter 6 by two new variables: redefine two old ones; and define one new parameter:

G ≡ physical gross investment
R ≡ physical replacement
X ≡ physical gross output
Y ≡ value of gross output
u ≡ useful life of a physical unit of capital stock

The Net Investment Function

Definitions

As before, define the proportionate rate of growth of variable v as

$$g_v \equiv \frac{dv}{dt} \frac{1}{v} \tag{8.1}$$

Define gross investment as the sum of net investment and replacement:

$$G \equiv I + R \tag{8.2}$$

Define net investment as the derivative of capital stock with respect to time:

$$I \equiv \frac{dS}{dt} \qquad (8.3)$$

Define replacement as what is necessary to make up for retirement. Let the useful life of a physical unit of capital stock be u. Then retirement at time τ is defined as gross investment at time $\tau - u$, and replacement is

$$R(\tau) \equiv G(\tau - u) \qquad (8.4)$$

Production

Let entrepreneurs apply a Cobb–Douglas production function

$$X = aL^{\alpha}S^{\beta} \qquad (8.5)$$

where $0 < \alpha < 1; 0 < \beta < 1; \alpha + \beta = 1;$ and $a > 0$. Let profit maximization under pure competition equalize real wage rate and physical marginal productivity of labor:

$$\frac{w}{P} = \frac{\partial X}{\partial L} = \alpha \frac{X}{L} \qquad (8.6)$$

Physical marginal productivity of capital stock is

$$\varkappa \equiv \frac{\partial X}{\partial S} = \beta \frac{X}{S} \qquad (8.7)$$

So far all equations look the same as before. But they do not mean the same. In our earlier chapters X stood for net output. Consequently multiplying equations like 8.7 by PS gave us profits $Z \equiv \varkappa PS = \beta PX$ *after* capital consumption allowances, and β was the share of such net profits in national money income. As we saw in chapter 4, Denison found that share to be $\beta = 0.20$.

In this chapter X stands for gross output. Consequently, multiplying equation 8.7 by PS would give us profits $Z \equiv \varkappa PS = \beta PX$ *before* capital consumption allowances, and β would be the share of such gross profits in gross national product. That share would be considerably higher than Denison's 0.20, say $\beta = 0.25$.

Investment Demand

Let N be the present net worth of new capital stock S installed by an entrepreneur. Let his desired capital stock be the size of stock maximizing present net worth. A first-order condition for a maximum is

$$n \equiv \frac{\partial N}{\partial S} = 0 \qquad (8.8)$$

To find desired capital stock proceed as follows. Let entrepreneurs be purely competitive ones, then price P of output is beyond their control. At time t, therefore, marginal value productivity of capital stock is $x(t)P(t)$, where in the definition 8.7 of x the X now stands for gross, not net, output. As seen from the present time τ, marginal value productivity at time t is $x(t)P(t)e^{-r(t-\tau)}$, where r is the stationary nominal rate of interest used as a discount rate. Define present gross worth of another physical unit of capital stock as the present worth of all future marginal value productivities over its entire useful life, now finite:

$$k(\tau) \equiv \int_{\tau}^{\tau+u} x(t)P(t)e^{-r(t-\tau)}dt \qquad (8.9)$$

Let entrepreneurs expect physical marginal productivity of capital stock to be growing at the stationary rate g_x:

$$x(t) = x(\tau)e^{g_x(t-\tau)} \qquad (8.10)$$

and price of output to be growing at the stationary rate g_P:

$$P(t) = P(\tau)e^{g_P(t-\tau)} \qquad (8.11)$$

Insert equations 8.10 and 8.11 into 8.9, define

$$\varrho \equiv r - (g_x + g_P) \qquad (8.12)$$

and write the integral 8.9 as

$$k(\tau) = \int_{\tau}^{\tau+u} x(\tau)P(\tau)e^{-\varrho(t-\tau)}dt \qquad (8.13)$$

Neither $x(\tau)$ nor $P(\tau)$ is a function of t, hence may be taken outside the integral sign. Our g_x, g_P, and r were all said to be stationary, hence the coefficient ϱ of t is stationary too. Assume $\varrho > 0$. As a result, find the integral to be

$$k = xP(1 - e^{-\varrho u})/\varrho \qquad (8.14)$$

where the function $(1 - e^{-\varrho u})/\varrho$ is mapped in figure 8-1.

Find present net worth of another physical unit of capital stock as its gross worth *minus* its price:

$$n \equiv k - P = [x(1 - e^{-\varrho u})/\varrho - 1]P \qquad (8.15)$$

Apply our first-order condition 8.8 to 8.15, find equilibrium physical marginal productivity of capital stock, and notice that it is no longer equal to the real rate of interest but larger: in addition to interest it should now cover capital consumption allowances.

$$x = \varrho/(1 - e^{-\varrho u}) \qquad (8.16)$$

Finally take equation 8.7 and 8.16 together and find desired capital stock

$$S = \beta X(1 - e^{-\varrho u})/\varrho \qquad (8.17)$$

Apply definitions 8.1 and 8.3 to equation 8.17 and find desired net investment as the derivative of desired capital stock with respect to time:

$$I \equiv \frac{dS}{dt} = \beta g_X X \frac{1 - e^{-\varrho u}}{\varrho} \qquad (8.18)$$

Equations 8.17 and 8.18 are capital stock and investment desired by an individual entrepreneur. As before, except X everything on the right–hand side of 8.17 and 8.18 is common to all entrepreneurs. Factor out all common factors, sum over all entrepreneurs, then X becomes gross national product, and 8.17 and 8.18 become national desired capital stock and net investment.

Notice that desired net investment is no longer in inverse proportion to ϱ: for a finite useful life u, when ϱ doubles the factor $(1 - e^{-\varrho u})/\varrho$, will not be cut in half but will be reduced less than that.

What is the effect of a longer useful life u upon desired net investment 8.18? The longer the useful life u, the closer the factor $(1 - e^{-\varrho u})/\varrho$ will come to being cut in half when ϱ doubles. And when u rises without bounds the factor $(1 - e^{-\varrho u})/\varrho$ approaches $1/\varrho$, and our new desired net investment function 8.18 approaches our old one, 6.16. It follows that investment in long–lived physical assets is more sensitive to the real rate of interest ϱ than is investment in short–lived ones. In figure 8-1, drawn in double–loga-

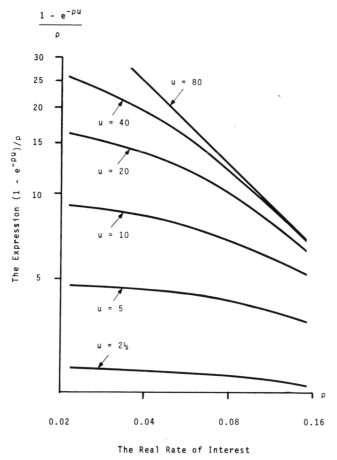

Figure 8-1. Mapping the Function $(1 - e^{-\varrho u})/\varrho$

rithmic scale, such sensitivity is measured by the steepness of the curves. And they are the steeper the longer the useful life u.

Consumption Demand

Let consumption remain a fixed proportion c of net output. Since our X is now gross rather than net output we must write our consumption function as

$$C = c(X - R) \qquad (8.19)$$

where $0 < c < 1$.

Goods-Market Equilibrium

In gross terms, too, goods-market equilibrium requires the supply of goods to equal the demand for them. But investment demand is now gross rather than net investment:

$$X = C + G \tag{8.20}$$

Gross National Product

With mortal capital stock the value of national output includes capital consumption allowances, hence is gross national product rather than national money income:

$$Y \equiv PX \tag{8.21}$$

Growth-Rate Solutions

No other revisions are called for. Equations specifying employment, the Phillips function, the demand for money, and the money-market equilibrium remain the same as in chapter 6. By taking derivatives with respect to time of all equations, new and old, the reader may convince himself that our gross system is satisfied by the growth-rate solutions 6.24 through 6.36 *plus* two new ones:

$$g_G = g_X \tag{8.22}$$

$$g_R = g_X \tag{8.23}$$

Having convinced ourselves that the growth-rate solutions 6.24 through 6.36 still hold, we may now use one of them, that is 6.26, to find the gross investment function.

The Gross Investment Function

The Gross-Net Investment Relationship

Under steady-state growth a particularly simple relationship will exist between gross and net investment. Let us find it.
    Insert equation 8.4 into 8.2 and write the latter

$$G(\tau) \equiv I(\tau) + G(\tau - u) \tag{8.24}$$

Going back q generations of capital stock, use equation 8.24 upon itself q times and find

$$G(\tau) \equiv I(\tau) + I(\tau - u) + ...$$
$$+ I(\tau - qu) + G[\tau - (q + 1)u] \qquad (8.25)$$

According to the growth-rate solution 6.26: $I(t) = I(\tau)e^{g_X(t-\tau)}$. Write this for $t = \tau, \tau - u, ..., \tau - qu$ and insert into equation 8.25:

$$G(\tau) = (1 + e^{-g_Xu} + ... + e^{-g_Xqu})I(\tau) + G[\tau - (q + 1)u]$$

The first parenthesis on the right-hand side is a geometric progression whose sum is

$$S_{q+1} = \frac{1 - e^{-g_X(q+1)u}}{1 - e^{-g_Xu}}$$

Let the number of generations of capital stock, q, rise without bounds. Then $G[\tau - (q + 1)u]$ will vanish. Since g_X and u are both positive,

$$\lim_{q \to \infty} G = I/(1 - e^{-g_Xu}) \qquad (8.26)$$

Equation 8.26 is the general gross-net investment relationship under steady-rate growth. If useful life, too, were to rise without bounds, the denominator $1 - e^{-g_Xu}$ would be approaching 1, and the entire right-hand side of 8.26 would be approaching I. We would, in other words, be approaching the special case of immortal capital stock, in which gross investment collapses into net investment.

The Gross Investment Function

Insert equation 8.18 into the limit 8.26 and find the gross investment function

$$\lim_{q \to \infty} G = \beta X \frac{1 - e^{-\varrho u}}{\varrho} \frac{g_X}{1 - e^{-g_Xu}} \qquad (8.27)$$

What is the effect of a longer useful life u upon desired gross investment 8.27? The effect is twofold. First, the net investment part 8.18 of 8.27 is up, as seen from figure 8-1. This is intuitively convincing: if at a given ϱ investments were longer-lived, more of them would be profitable and undertaken. Second, the replacement part of equation 8.27 is down. For a given g_X the denominator $1 - e^{-g_Xu}$ is the greater the longer is u. This, too, is intuitively convincing: if at a given rate of growth g_X investments were longer-lived, current replacement 8.4 would be the gross investment of a more distant past. And in a growing economy the gross investment of a more distant past must be smaller than the gross investment of a more recent one.

The Real Rate of Interest

Insert solutions 6.27 and 6.33, still valid, into our definition 8.12 and find that ϱ is still the real rate of interest:

$$\varrho = r - g_P \tag{8.28}$$

Can we solve for ϱ? Insert equation 8.2 into 8.20 and the result into 8.19, thus expressing consumption in terms of net investment:

$$C = cI/(1 - c) \tag{8.29}$$

Use equation 8.18 to express gross national product in terms of net investment and 8.26 to express gross in terms of net investment. Now we have expressed all three terms of 8.20 in terms of net investment. Divide both sides of 8.20 by net investment and find

$$\frac{1 - e^{-\varrho u}}{\varrho} = \frac{1/\beta}{cg_X/(1 - c) + g_X/(1 - e^{-g_X u})} \tag{8.30}$$

Equation 8.30 is not an explicit solution for ϱ, but figure 8-1 helps us to see its Fisherian properties. In a thrifty economy c will be low, which makes the right-hand side of 8.30 high. For the left-hand side to be high as well, figure 8-1 shows that ϱ must be low, as Fisher said. In a rapidly growing economy g_X will be high, which makes the right-hand side of 8.30 low: for a high g_X the ratio $g_X/(1 - e^{-g_X u})$ is high. For the left-hand side to be low as well, figure 8-1 shows that ϱ must be high, as Fisher said. Our theoretical results of chapter 6 still stand!

Numerical Illustration

The main results of this chapter are equations 8.18, 8.27, and 8.30. Into them let us insert the empirically plausible parameter values:

$$\beta = 0.25 \qquad g_X = 0.03$$
$$1 - c = 0.09 \qquad u = 25$$

Insert those values into 8.30 and find $(1 - e^{-\varrho u})/\varrho = 11.1$. Consult figure 8-1 or a table of powers of e and find the corresponding real rate of interest $\varrho = 0.077$, a bit on the high side. Insert into equation 8.18 and find the net-investment to gross-output ratio $I/X = 0.083$, a not implausible value. Insert into our limit 8.27 and find the gross-investment to gross-output ratio $G/X = 0.158$, a not implausible value.

Conclusion

What difference, if any, did it make to growth rates, investment, and interest rates if capital stock were mortal?

To growth rates it made no difference at all. All the growth rates 6.24 through 6.36 still stand. Specifically, then, the rate of growth of the real wage rate $g_w - g_P$ still stands and is the same for any value of the employment fraction λ and the inflationary potential p. Friedman's natural rate of unemployment is not unique in our gross economy either.

A very simple relationship 8.26 was found to exist between gross and net investment. A solution for the real rate of interest was found. Its mathematics became slightly more involved but its properties were still those found in chapter 6.

Perhaps such slight complications were a price worth paying for moving one step closer to gross national accounting data, usually considered more accurate than net ones.

Reference

E.F. Denison, *Accounting for United States Economic Growth 1929-1969,* Washington, D.C., 1974.

9

Nature and Growth: Exhaustible and Nonexhaustible Natural Resources

The evidence on substitutability is not yet definitive but what there is suggests a large degree of substitutability between exhaustible resources and renewable or reproducible resources.

U.S., National Commission
on Supplies and Shortages (1976: 19).

Chapters 4 through 8 found steady-state growth to be possible. But such growth is explosive: a newly independent nation growing at a rate as moderate as 3 percent per annum will be 403 times larger when it celebrates its bicentennial.

By contrast, a nonexhaustible natural resource like land is stationary, and an exhaustible one like fossil fuels is being absorbed in the production process. Must something growing without bound eventually swamp anything stationary or even dwindling?

Growth optimism based on geological and technological potential merely asserts that what is finite is very large indeed. But neither geology nor technology alone can remove the logical conflict between finite resources and growth without bounds. Only economics can do that, and this chapter will try to do it. We shall assume, first, growing technology; second, growing labor force; third, steady-state dwindling extraction of minerals making useful life of mines rise without bounds; and fourth, that man-made and natural resources are good albeit not perfect substitutes. We shall then demonstrate that steady-state growth of physical output and the real wage rate is both feasible and profitable. Contrary to popular beliefs we shall find immiserization to be a very remote possibility in advanced economies but perhaps a distinct one in backward preindustrial economies.

Notation

Let us expand the notation of chapter 6 by six new variables, and one new parameter:

k ≡ present gross worth of mine
Q ≡ existing physical quantity of mineral
q ≡ physical quantity of mineral extracted per unit of time

u ≡ useful life of mine
V ≡ money rent bill of mine
v ≡ money rent rate of mine
γ ≡ elasticity of output of goods with respect to input of mineral

On Mining

Existing Natural Resources

Write an inventory of all existing natural resources as the vector Q. Within economic time, short enough to exclude geological change, the derivative with respect to time of any element of Q must be nonpositive. If, like agricultural land or waterfalls generating hydroelectric power, the element is being used without being extracted, the derivative is zero. That case will be considered at the end of this chapter. If, like fossil fuels, the element is being extracted, the derivative is negative. This is the case considered in the bulk of this chapter.

Extraction

Define extraction as

$$q \equiv -\frac{dQ}{dt} \tag{9.1}$$

which, within economic time, will then be nonnegative. Accumulated extraction from time τ to time $\tau + u$ is

$$\int_{\tau}^{\tau+u} q(t)\,dt \tag{9.2}$$

Let extraction be growing at the stationary rate g_q:

$$q(t) = q(\tau)e^{g_q(t-\tau)} \tag{9.3}$$

Insert equation 9.3 into 9.2 and write the latter as

$$\int_{\tau}^{\tau+u} q(\tau)e^{g_q(t-\tau)}\,dt \tag{9.4}$$

Here $q(\tau)$ is not a function of t, hence may be taken outside the integral sign. The growth rate g_q was said to be stationary, hence the coefficient of t is stationary. As a result, find the integral to be

$$q(\tau)(e^{g_q u} - 1)/g_q \tag{9.5}$$

Useful Life of Mine

The physical quantity of the mineral remaining at time $\tau + u$ is defined as the physical quantity remaining at time τ *minus* the accumulated extraction from time τ to time $\tau + u$:

$$Q(\tau + u) \equiv Q(\tau) - q(\tau)(e^{g_q u} - 1)/g_q \qquad (9.6)$$

The useful life of the mine is defined as that value of u at which the physical quantity of the mineral remaining becomes zero. Set equation 9.6 equal to zero, strip $Q(\tau)$ and $q(\tau)$ of their time coordinate, and arrive at the transcendental equation

$$e^{g_q u} = 1 + g_q Q/q \qquad (9.7)$$

According to equation 9.1 extraction q was nonnegative. Let us dismiss the case $q = 0$ of a dormant mine and confine ourselves to the case $q > 0$ of a working one. Then in our transcendental equation 9.7 let us distinguish three cases.

Positive Growth of Extraction

If the growth rate of extraction is positive, $g_q > 0$, may useful life u of a mine rise without bounds? If it did, the left-hand side of equation 9.7 would rise without bounds. The right-hand side could do the same if and only if q could vanish. But with $g_q > 0$ and $q > 0$ that is impossible: extraction q must be growing rather than vanishing. We conclude that u must be finite.

Zero Growth of Extraction

If the growth rate of extraction is zero, $g_q = 0$, our form 9.5 is undefined, and our transcendental equation 9.7 cannot be derived from it. Instead we must insert $g_q = 0$ into our form 9.4 and find our integral 9.2 to be

$$\int_\tau^{\tau + u} q(\tau)dt = q(\tau)\int_\tau^{\tau + u} 1dt = q(\tau)u \qquad (9.8)$$

Now equation 9.6 will be

$$Q(\tau + u) \equiv Q(\tau) - q(\tau)u \qquad (9.9)$$

Set equation 9.9 equal to zero, strip its right-hand side of the time coordinate τ, and find the nontranscendental equation

$$u = Q/q \tag{9.10}$$

Now may useful life u rise without bounds? If it did, the left-hand side of equation 9.10 would rise without bounds. The right-hand side could do the same if and only if q could vanish. But with $g_q = 0$ and $q > 0$ that is impossible: extraction q must be stationary rather than vanishing. We conclude that u must be finite.

Negative Growth of Extraction

If the growth rate of extraction is negative, $g_q < 0$, may useful life u rise without bounds? If it did, the left-hand side of equation 9.7 would vanish. The right-hand side could do the same if and only if

$$g_q = -q/Q \tag{9.11}$$

With $g_q < 0$ and $q > 0$ that is entirely possible. In order to take the integral 9.2 we assumed g_q to be stationary. For that to be true, the numerator and the denominator of equation 9.11 must be growing at the same, negative, rate

$$g_q = g_Q \tag{9.12}$$

So there will be steady-state, albeit negative, growth of both extraction and existing physical quantity of the mineral. Of the latter there will always be some left: the mine will never be empty. Let us fit this result into the growth model set out in chapter 6.

**Exhaustible Natural Resources in a
Neoclassical Growth Model**

Production

Let the mineral be an input in a Cobb-Douglas production function

$$X = aL^{\alpha}S^{\beta}q^{\gamma} \tag{9.13}$$

where $0 < \alpha < 1$; $0 < \beta < 1$; $0 < \gamma < 1$; $\alpha + \beta + \gamma = 1$; and $a > 0$. Let the price per ton of mineral be v. Profit maximization under pure competition in the market for output will then equalize the real price and the physical marginal productivity of the mineral:

$$\frac{v}{P} = \frac{\partial X}{\partial q} = \gamma \frac{X}{q} \tag{9.14}$$

The Money Rent Bill

Consider the having-your-cake-or-eating-it problem in its purest form. Ignore cost[a] of extraction, then the money rent rate of the mine, that is, the money rent per ton of mineral, equals the price of the mineral. Multiply equation 9.14 by Pq and express the money rent bill as the money value of extraction:

$$V \equiv qv = \gamma PX \tag{9.15}$$

National Money Income after Depletion Allowance

Speaking of the "rent of coal mines, and of stone quarries," Ricardo (1817, ch. 2) observed that such rent "is paid for the value of the coal or stone which can be removed from them, and has no connnection with the original and indestructible powers of the land." Consequently such rent is not income but a depletion allowance. National money income after depletion allowance is

$$Y \equiv PX - V = (1 - \gamma)PX \tag{9.16}$$

Consumption

Let consumption be the fixed proportion c of national real income after depletion allowance:

$$C = cY/P = c(1 - \gamma)X \tag{9.17}$$

---

[a]Cost and diminishing returns in extraction are practically important and are emphasized in the literature from Cassel (1923) and Hotelling (1931) to Solow (1974), Solow and Wan (1976), and Pindyck (1978). Whether or not diminishing returns at a moment of time are offset by technological progress was examined by Nordhaus (1974: 24), who found the historical *labor* cost of resources to have been declining. Goeller and Weinberg (1978: 7) examined the *energy* cost of resources and found the estimated energy required to produce metals from essentially inexhaustible sources to be not more than 60 percent higher than the energy required to win metals from high-grade ores.

Is Steady–State Growth of the Economy Feasible?

Convergence

We modify the convergence proof of chapter 6 to allow for exhaustible natural resources. Insert equation 6.19, where λ is not a function of time, into our production function 9.13, differentiate the latter with respect to time, and express the proportionate rate of growth of physical output

$$g_X = g_a + \alpha g_F + \beta g_S + \gamma g_q \qquad (9.18)$$

Use equations 6.18, 6.2, and 6.1 in that order, use our new consumption function 9.17, and express the proportionate rate of growth of physical capital stock

$$g_S = [1 - c(1 - \gamma)]X/S \qquad (9.19)$$

Differentiate equation 9.19 with respect to time, use 6.1 and 9.18, and express the proportionate rate of acceleration of physical capital stock

$$g_{gS} = (\alpha + \gamma)[(g_a + \alpha g_F + \gamma g_q)/(\alpha + \gamma) - g_S] \qquad (9.20)$$

In equation 9.20 there are three possibilities: if $g_S > (g_a + \alpha g_F + \gamma g_q)/(\alpha + \gamma)$, then $g_{gS} < 0$. If

$$g_S = (g_a + \alpha g_F + \gamma g_q)/(\alpha + \gamma) \qquad (9.21)$$

then $g_{gS} = 0$. Finally, if $g_S < (g_a + \alpha g_F + \gamma g_q)/(\alpha + \gamma)$, then $g_{gS} > 0$. Consequently, if greater than equation 9.21 g_S is falling; if equal to 9.21 g_S is stationary; and if less than 9.21 g_S is rising. Furthermore, g_S cannot alternate around 9.21, for differential equations trace continuous time paths, and as soon as a g_S-path touched 9.21 it would have to stay there. Finally, g_S cannot converge to anything else than 9.21, for if it did, by letting enough time elapse we could make the left–hand side of 9.20 smaller than any arbitrarily assignable positive constant ϵ, however small, without the same being possible for the right–hand side. We conclude that g_S must either equal 9.21 from the outset or, if it does not, converge to that value.

Other Growth Rates

Insert equation 9.21 into 9.18 and find the growth rate of physical output

$$g_X = g_S = (g_a + \alpha g_F + \gamma g_q)/(\alpha + \gamma) \qquad (9.22)$$

Take the derivative of equation 6.4 with respect to time. Insert equations 6.20, 6.28, and 9.22 and find our price–wage equilibrium solutions

$$g_P = \frac{p(1 - \lambda)^\pi}{1 - \Phi} - \frac{g_a - \gamma(g_F - g_q)}{(1 - \Phi)(\alpha + \gamma)} \tag{9.23}$$

$$g_w = \frac{p(1 - \lambda)^\pi}{1 - \Phi} - \Phi\frac{g_a - \gamma(g_F - g_q)}{(1 - \Phi)(\alpha + \gamma)} \tag{9.24}$$

$$g_{w/P} = g_w - g_P = [g_a - \gamma(g_F - g_q)]/(\alpha + \gamma) \tag{9.25}$$

So once again the employment fraction λ and the inflationary potential p disappeared from the rate of growth of the real wage rate: Friedman's natural rate of unemployment is still not unique!

Differentiate equations 9.15 and 9.16 with respect to time, insert 6.36, and find the rate of growth of the money rent bill

$$g_V = g_Y = g_P + g_X = g_F + g_w \tag{9.26}$$

For the values, perhaps not unrealistic,

$$\begin{aligned}
\alpha &= 0.75 \\
g_a &= 0.02 \\
g_F &= 0.01 \\
\gamma &= 0.05 \\
p(1 - \lambda)^\pi &= 0.05 \\
\Phi &= 0.50
\end{aligned}$$

Figure 9-1 shows g_X, g_P, g_w, $g_{w/P}$, and g_V as functions of g_q.

Is Steady-State Growth of the Economy Feasible?

For four reasons the growth rate 9.22 of output may easily be positive: first, a technology growing at the positive rate g_a; second, a labor force growing at the positive rate g_F; third, steady-state growth of extraction at a negative rate making useful life u of mines rise without bounds; and fourth, a production function 9.13 in which man–made and natural resources are good albeit not perfect substitutes.

Natural Resources and Inflation

Are dwindling natural resources a cause of inflation? Certainly: the rate of inflation 9.23 is the higher the more rapidly they are dwindling. Rapidly

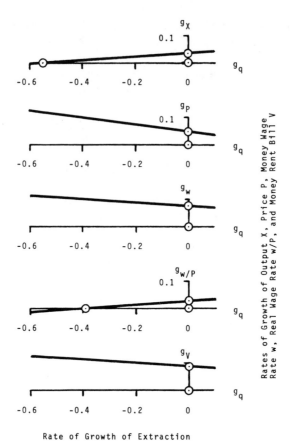

Figure 9-1. Growth Rates of Output, Price, Money and Real Wage Rates, and Money Rent Bill as Functions of the Growth Rate of Extraction

dwindling natural resources mean a low, that is, numerically high g_q, and the derivative $\partial g_P / \partial g_q$ of equation 9.23 is negative.

Interest Rates

Allowing for our new consumption function 9.17, we replace equation 6.37 by

$$[1 - c(1 - \gamma)]X = I \qquad (9.27)$$

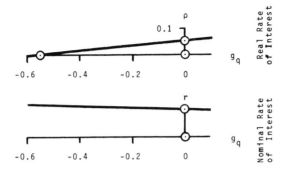

Rate of Growth of Extraction

Figure 9-2. Real and Nominal Rates of Interest as Functions of the Growth Rate of Extraction

Insert equation 9.27 into 6.16, still valid, and find the real rate of interest

$$\varrho = \beta g_X/[1 - c(1 - \gamma)] \tag{9.28}$$

where g_X stands for our solution 9.22. Insert equation 9.28 into definition 6.38, still valid, and find the nominal rate of interest

$$r = \beta g_X/[1 - c(1 - \gamma)] + g_P \tag{9.29}$$

where g_P and g_X stand for our solutions 9.23 and 9.22, respectively.

For the values of parameters used above and for $c = 0.91$ figure 9-2 shows ϱ and r as functions of g_q.

Is Steady–State Growth of the Economy Profitable?

It is not enough to show that steady–state growth of the economy is feasible. We must also show that it is profitable. We do that by finding the present gross worth of a mine.

Present Gross Worth of a Mine

At time t the money rent bill is $V(t)$. As seen from the present time τ, the money rent bill at time t is $V(t)e^{-r(t-\tau)}$, where r is the stationary nominal rate of interest used as a discount rate. Define present gross worth of the mine as the present worth of all its future money rent bills over its entire useful life:

$$k(\tau) \equiv \int_{\tau}^{\tau+u} V(t)e^{-r(t-\tau)}dt \qquad (9.30)$$

Let the mine owner expect the money rent bill to be growing at the stationary rate g_V:

$$V(t) = V(\tau)e^{g_V(t-\tau)} \qquad (9.31)$$

Insert equation 9.31 into 9.30, define

$$\omega \equiv r - g_V \qquad (9.32)$$

and write the integral 9.30 as

$$k(\tau) = \int_{\tau}^{\tau+u} V(\tau)e^{-\omega(t-\tau)}dt$$

$V(\tau)$ is not a function of t, hence may be taken outside the integral sign. Our g_V and r were said to be stationary, hence the coefficient ω of t is stationary, too. As a result, find the integral to be

$$k = V(1 - e^{-\omega u})/\omega \qquad (9.33)$$

Let us distinguish three possibilities. If $\omega < 0$ the rate of growth g_V of the money rent bill exceeds the discount rate r. As a result, discounted future money rent bills are the larger the more distant they are, and k is a sum of u rising terms.

If $\omega = 0$ and u were finite, the present gross worth 9.33 would be undefined. But we can find the limit of 9.33 by applying L'Hôpital's rule:

$$\lim_{\omega \to 0} k = \lim_{\omega \to 0} \frac{\partial[V(1 - e^{-\omega u})]/\partial \omega}{\partial \omega / \partial \omega} = \lim_{\omega \to 0} Vue^{-\omega u} = Vu$$

In this case the rate of growth g_V of the money rent bill equals the discount rate r. As a result, discounted future money rent bills are now the same regardless of their distance from the present, and k is a sum of u identical terms, each worth V.

Finally, if $\omega > 0$ the rate of growth g_V of the money rent bill falls short of the discount rate r. As a result, discounted future money rent bills are the smaller the more distant they are, and k is a sum of u dwindling terms.

Which of the three possibilities is the true one? Insert equations 9.26 and 9.29 into 9.32 and find

$$\omega = \{\beta - [1 - c(1 - \gamma)]\}g_X/[1 - c(1 - \gamma)] \qquad (9.34)$$

For the not unrealistic values of parameters used above and for $c = 0.91$, β will easily exceed $1 - c(1 - \gamma)$, hence our third possibility $\omega > 0$ is the true one.

Is Steady-State Growth of the Economy More Profitable?

This chapter is considering the having-your-cake-or-eating-it problem in its purest form: as we saw above, if the growth rate of extraction is positive or zero, $g_q \geq 0$, useful life u of mines must be finite, and the cake will be gone after a finite time. But as we also saw, if the growth rate of extraction is negative, $g_q < 0$, useful life u may rise without bounds, and there will always be some cake left. Which of the two alternatives will make present worth 9.33 greater?

In equation 9.33 we find, first, the current money rent bill V. Insert equation 6.19 into 6.4, find $PX = \lambda Fw/\alpha$, insert that into 9.15, and find the current money rent bill

$$V = \gamma\lambda Fw/\alpha \qquad (9.35)$$

Nothing in equation 9.35 is a function of g_q. In 9.33 we find, next, the function $(1 - e^{-\omega u})/\omega$, mapped for $\omega > 0$ in our double-logarithmic figure 9-3. In 9.34 g_X stands for our solution 9.22, consequently according to 9.34 ω is a function of g_q. To find how ω depends upon g_q take the derivative of 9.34 with 9.22 inserted and find

$$\frac{\partial \omega}{\partial g_q} = \frac{\beta - [1 - c(1 - \gamma)]}{1 - c(1 - \gamma)} \frac{\gamma}{\alpha + \gamma} \qquad (9.36)$$

As we saw, β will easily exceed $1 - c(1 - \gamma)$, hence equation 9.36 is positive. Consequently, if the growth rate of extraction is positive or zero, $g_q \geq 0$, the mine owner will be facing a higher ω than if the growth rate of extraction is negative, $g_q < 0$. He will also be facing a finite useful life u rather than one rising without bounds. For both reasons his present worth 9.33 will be down: figure 9-3 shows $(1 - e^{-\omega u})/\omega$ to be down if at the same time ω is up and u is down.

In other words, growth interrupted by empty mines is less profitable

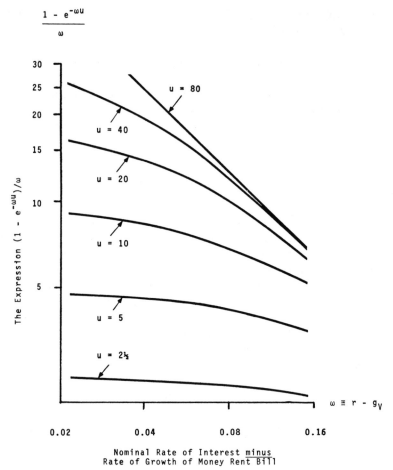

Figure 9-3. Mapping the Function $(1 - e^{-\omega u})/\omega$

than steady-state growth of the economy at a useful life of mines rising
without bounds. Indeed, growth interrupted by empty mines would be a
physical disaster. If there were no extraction physical output would drop to
zero: if in equation 9.13 $q = 0$, $X = 0$.

Being more profitable, steady-state growth will prevail and validate the
constraint $g_q < 0$ under which figure 9-1 and 9-2 were drawn. But if u rises
without bounds and $\omega > 0$, present worth 9.33 collapses into

$$k = V/\omega \qquad\qquad (9.37)$$

Immiserization in Advanced and Preindustrial Economies

Advanced Economy: A Jevonian Race

Modern energy worries are not so modern. The first industrial revolution was based on the steam engine, the steam engine was based on coal, and in 1866 Jevons published his *Coal Question* predicting an early exhaustion of Britain's coal deposits.

Our solution 9.25 for the rate of growth of the real wage rate may be read as a Jevonian technology-population race under exhaustible natural resources. The higher the rate of technological progress g_a the higher the rate of growth of the real wage rate $g_{w/P}$. But from g_a in 9.25 we must deduct the term $\gamma(g_F - g_q)$. Because g_F is nonnegative and g_q negative, the parenthesis is positive and is the larger the more rapidly the labor force is growing and the more rapidly natural resources are dwindling. The coefficient of the parenthesis is the elasticity γ and is the larger the more important are the natural resources. Technology will lose the race, and the rate of growth of the real wage rate become negative, if the labor force is growing rapidly enough, if natural resources are dwindling rapidly enough, and if they are important enough. Are they?

How Large Is γ In an Advanced Economy?

In a purely competitive economy in which nature's exponent in a Cobb–Douglas production function were γ, the share of national output imputed to nature in the form of rent would be γ; compare equation 9.15. Observe two implications. First, "nature" would include merely what is exploitable under existing technology. Second, nature would include merely land and what lies beneath it, for only land and what lies beneath it can be subject to private property and draw rent. With these two implications Nordhaus and Tobin (1972) found γ to be around 0.05 in the United States.

The Outcome of the Race

Inserting the parameter values used above into our solution 9.25, we find the rate of growth of the real wage rate in an advanced economy using primarily exhaustible natural resources growing at, say, -0.06 per annum: $g_{w/P} = 0.0206$, which, as we saw in chapter 4, is about what Phelps Brown found for the United States 1890/99–1960. Figure 9-1 shows that the rate of growth of extraction g_q would have to be numerically very high—and very unrealistic—in order to choke off the growth of the real wage rate. We conclude that in an advanced economy like the United States immiserization is a very remote possibility.

Preindustrial Economy

In a preindustrial economy, as Cantillon, Smith, Malthus, and Ricardo knew it and most of mankind know it today, energy is provided primarily by human and animal muscle power. Food and feed are nature's most prominent gifts to man, and they are grown on a nonexhaustible natural resource, agricultural land. What would our technology–population race look like under nonexhaustible natural resources?

Our model of exhaustible resources collapses readily into the special case of nonexhaustible ones. All we need is to redefine our q, V, and v. Our q is no longer extraction but the quantity of service rendered by the nonexhaustible natural resource and measured in, say, acre–years rendered per year. The service rendered remains stationary, because the natural resource does. Consequently

$$g_q = 0 \qquad (9.38)$$

Our V is still a money rent bill, our v a money rent rate, and $V \equiv qv$. But our V is no longer a Ricardian rent of mines, a depletion allowance. V is now a Ricardian rent of land, a payment for the "original and indestructible powers of land." Our v is no longer the price of the mineral extracted but that of the service rendered and measured in, say, dollars per acre–year.

To find our new growth rates of output X, capital stock S, price P, money wage rate w, real wage rate w/P, and money rent bill V, we insert equation 9.38 into our solutions 9.22 through 9.26 and find the latter collapsing into

$$g_X = g_S = (g_a + \alpha g_F)/(\alpha + \gamma) \qquad (9.39)$$

$$g_P = \frac{p(1 - \lambda)^\pi}{1 - \Phi} - \frac{g_a - \gamma g_F}{(1 - \Phi)(\alpha + \gamma)} \qquad (9.40)$$

$$g_w = \frac{p(1 - \lambda)^\pi}{1 - \Phi} - \Phi \frac{g_a - \gamma g_F}{(1 - \Phi)(\alpha + \gamma)} \qquad (9.41)$$

$$g_{w/P} = g_w - g_P = (g_a - \gamma g_F)/(\alpha + \gamma) \qquad (9.42)$$

$$g_V = g_P + g_X = g_F + g_w \qquad (9.43)$$

A Ricardian Race

Our solution 9.42 for the rate of growth of the real wage rate may be read as a Ricardian technology-population race under nonexhaustible natural resources. The higher the rate of technological progress g_a the higher the rate of growth of the real wage rate $g_{w/P}$. But from g_a in 9.42 we must deduct the term γg_F, which is nonnegative. Its coefficient is the elasticity γ and is the larger the more important are the natural resources. Technology will lose the Ricardian race, and the rate of growth of the real wage rate become negative, if the labor force is growing rapidly enough and if natural resources are important enough. Are they?

How Large Is γ in a Preindustrial Economy?

The exponent γ may be 0.05 in the United States. But in preindustrial economies it must be much higher. From the past of our own industrial economies Kuznets (1971: 67) cites evidence that land and subsoil assets were between ⅓ and ½ of total wealth: Deane and Cole found it to be over ½ in Great Britain in 1798, 1812, and 1832; Goldsmith found it to be about ½ in the United States in 1805; Falbe–Hansen found it to be 0.44 in Denmark in 1880; and Fahlbeck found it to be 0.42 in Sweden in 1885. Furthermore Walters (1963: 32-33) reports on estimates of modern agricultural production functions for advanced and preindustrial economies alike. Japan and Iowa had γ's higher than ½; all other areas reported on had γ's between ¼ and ½. For a preindustrial economy we might, perhaps, guess the following:

$$\alpha = 0.60$$
$$g_a = 0.01$$
$$g_F = 0.03$$
$$\gamma = 0.20$$

A preindustrial economy may make no contribution of its own to the rate of technological progress g_a. But we have assumed it to be capable of absorbing one-half of the technological progress originating elsewhere.

The Outcome of the Race

Inserting these values into our solution 9.42 we find the growth rate of the real wage rate in a preindustrial economy using primarily nonexhaustible natural resources: $g_{w/P} = 0.005$, or one-half of 1 percent. If the rate of technological progress g_a had been slightly lower than 0.01 or if population growth had been somewhat higher than 0.03 the rate of growth of the real wage rate could have become negative. We conclude that in backward pre-industrial economies like Bangladesh immiserization is a distinct possibility: man could lose the Ricardian race.

Marx

Couldn't Marx have used such a lost Ricardian race to salvage his immiserization hypothesis? Wasn't he, as Samuelson (1957: 911) put it, "a minor post-Ricardian"? He was, but he had thrown away the one Ricardian building block which could have salvaged, at least logically, his immiserization hypothesis. Marxian production functions have labor and capital in them but no land. As Samuelson (1957: 884) also said, Marx can be classified as "Ricardo without diminishing returns." Marx's γ was zero. But if in our equations 9.25 or 9.42 γ were zero, labor and natural resources would have been disqualified from any Jevonian or Ricardian race. Left with no contestants technology would win, and there could be no immiserization.

Conclusions

Neither geology nor technology alone can remove the logical conflict between finite resources and growth without bounds. Only economics can do that, and we have tried to do it.

Assuming, first, growing technology; second, growing labor force; third, steady-state dwindling extraction of minerals making useful life of mines rise without bounds; and fourth, that man-made and natural resources are good albeit not perfect substitutes; we have demonstrated that steady-state growth of physical output and the real wage rate was both feasible and profitable.

Dwindling natural resources could be one of the causes of inflation: our solution for the rate of inflation was found to be the higher the more rapidly natural resources were dwindling.

Contrary to popular beliefs, immiserization would be a remote possibility in advanced economies but perhaps a distinct one in backward preindustrial economies.

References

G. Cassel, *Theoretische Sozialökonomie,* Erlangen and Leipzig 1923, VII, Sec. 31, 267–274.

H.E. Goeller and A.M. Weinberg, "The Age of Substitutability," *Amer. Econ. Rev.*, Dec. 1978, *68*, 1–11.

H. Hotelling, "The Economics of Exhaustible Resources, *J. Polit. Econ.*, Apr. 1931, *39*, 137–175.

W.S. Jevons, *The Coal Question*, London 1866.

S. Kuznets, *Economic Growth of Nations*, Cambridge, Mass. 1971.

W.D. Nordhaus, "Resources as a Constraint on Growth," *Amer. Econ. Rev.*, May 1974, *64*, 22–26.

W.D. Nordhaus and J. Tobin, "Is Economic Growth Obsolete?" National Bureau of Economic Research, *Economic Growth*, New York 1972.

R.S. Pindyck, "The Optimal Exploration and Production of Nonrenewable Resources," *J. Polit. Econ.*, Oct. 1978, *86*, 841–861.

D. Ricardo, *The Principles of Political Economy and Taxation*, London 1817.

P.A. Samuelson, "Wages and Interest: A Modern Dissection of Marxian Economic Models," *Amer. Econ. Rev.*, Dec. 1957, *47*, 884–912.

R.M. Solow, "The Economics of Resources or the Resources of Economics," *Amer. Econ. Rev.*, May 1974, *64*, 1–14.

R.M. Solow and F.Y. Wan, "Extraction Costs in the Theory of Exhaustible Resources," *Bell J. Econ.*, Autumn 1976, *7*, 359–370.

U.S. Government, National Commission on Supplies and Shortages, *Government and the Nation's Resources*, Washington, D.C., 1976.

A.A. Walters, "Production and Cost Functions: An Econometric Survey," *Econometrica*, Jan.-Apr. 1963, *31*, 1–66.

10 Two Goods: Steady-State but Unbalanced Growth

Smaller-scale [maps] require heavier generalization of the forms of the terrain.... Simplifying, summarizing, and omitting appropriately is a very important job.... Too much is as harmful as too little.

Translated from Landesvermessungsamt
Schleswig-Holstein (1963: 188)

Like maps, theory is a simplified picture of reality. Typical simplifications are a closed economy, pure competition, perfect foresight, and steady-state growth. Like highway maps, U.S. Geological Survey maps, and nautical maps, different theories serve different purposes.

For purposes such as simulating convergence to steady-state growth of output, identical steady-state growth rates of output and capital stock, stationary rate of return to capital, identical steady-state growth rates of the real wage rate and labor productivity, and stationary distributive shares, the one-good neoclassical model may be adequate, as we saw in chapter 4. Wicksell, Keynes, and monetarists may even coexist in it, as we saw in chapter 6. If so, so much the better: economists, too, should economize!

But the one-good neoclassical model can simulate neither realistic steady-state but unbalanced growth nor realistic resource allocation involving substitution among different goods in consumption as well as production.

To allow for unbalanced growth a growth model needs at least two goods. But to allow for the full resource allocation it will not do to let those goods be merely the consumers' good and the producers' good found in Ricardo, Marx, and the usual Uzawa (1961) two-sector growth models. With only one consumers' good, such models are still models of homogeneous consumption, permitting no substitution among consumers' goods and asking no question, hence offering no answer, concerning the allocation of consumption expenditure among consumers' goods. With only one producers' good, such models are still models of homogeneous capital stock, permitting no substitution among producers' goods and asking no question, hence offering no answer, concerning the allocation of investment expenditure among producers' goods.

We wish to build the simplest possible growth model of heterogeneous consumption as well as capital stock, thus allowing for the full allocation of resources. Can we do it? Post-Keynesians think that we cannot build a neoclassical one, because a multigood physical capital stock cannot be expressed as a single number.

It surely cannot, but who needs a single number? Let us extend the one-good model of chapter 6 to two goods. Let *each* of them serve interchangeably as a consumers' or a producers' good, just as the single good did in chapter 6. Let physical output of the jth good be X_j, where $j \equiv 1, 2$. Let the jth good be produced from labor L_j and two immortal physical capital stocks S_{ij}, where $i \equiv 1, 2$. So there are four physical capital stocks S_{ij} having four physical marginal productivities $\varkappa_{ij}$. Physical capital stock and its physical marginal productivity remain meaningful as matrices and operational in the sense that they help us find explicit, positive, and real solutions for all variables.

Notation

Variables

$C \equiv$ physical consumption
$D \equiv$ demand for money
$g_v \equiv$ proportionate rate of growth of variable $v \equiv C, D, I, \varkappa, L, M, P, r, \varrho,$
    $S, w, X,$ and Y
$I \equiv$ physical investment
$k \equiv$ present gross worth of another physical unit of capital stock
$\varkappa \equiv$ physical marginal productivity of capital stock
$L \equiv$ labor employed
$\lambda \equiv$ proportion employed of available labor force
$M \equiv$ supply of money
$N \equiv$ present net worth of entire physical capital stock
$n \equiv$ present net worth of another physical unit of capital stock
$P \equiv$ price of goods
$p \equiv$ one coefficient of Phillips function representing inflationary potential
$r \equiv$ nominal rate of interest
$\varrho \equiv$ real rate of interest
$S \equiv$ physical capital stock
$U \equiv$ utility
$w \equiv$ money wage rate
$X \equiv$ physical output
$Y \equiv$ money income

Parameters

$a \quad \equiv$ multiplicative factor of production function
$\alpha, \beta \equiv$ exponents of production function

c ≡ propensity to consume money income
F ≡ available labor force
g_v ≡ proportionate rate of growth of parameter $v \equiv a$ and F
m ≡ multiplicative factor of demand for money function
μ ≡ exponent of demand for money function
π ≡ exponent of Phillips function
u ≡ multiplicative factor of utility function
v ≡ exponent of utility function

All parameters are stationary except a and F, whose growth rates are stationary. Time coordinates are t for general time and τ for specific time. Euler's number e is the base of natural logarithms. G, H, J, and K stand for agglomerations to be defined as we go along.

The Model

Definitions

Define the proportionate rate of growth

$$g_v \equiv \frac{dv}{dt}\frac{1}{v} \tag{10.1}$$

Define investment as the derivative of capital stock with respect to time:

$$I_{ij} \equiv \frac{dS_{ij}}{dt} \tag{10.2}$$

Production

For its production each good needs capital stock of both goods. The output X_j of the jth good is produced from labor L_j and two immortal capital stocks S_{ij}, where i is the sector of origin and j the sector of installation. As a result, there are four distinct physical capital stocks S_{ij} in the model. Let every entrepreneur have access to a Cobb–Douglas production function

$$X_1 = a_1 L_1^{\alpha_1}\ S_{11}^{\beta_{11}}\ S_{21}^{\beta_{21}} \tag{10.3}$$

$$X_2 = a_2 L_2^{\alpha_2}\ S_{12}^{\beta_{12}}\ S_{22}^{\beta_{22}} \tag{10.4}$$

where $0 < \alpha_j < 1; 0 < \beta_{ij} < 1; \alpha_1 + \beta_{11} + \beta_{21} = 1; \alpha_2 + \beta_{12} + \beta_{22} = 1;$ and $a_j > 0$. Assume a fairly strong interindustry dependence: let each industry be at least as dependent upon the capital stock supplied by the other as upon that supplied by itself, then $\beta_{11} \leq \beta_{21}$, $\beta_{22} \leq \beta_{12}$.

In each industry let profit maximization under pure competition equalize real wage rate and physical marginal productivity of labor:

$$\frac{w}{P_i} = \frac{\partial X_i}{\partial L_i} = \alpha_i \frac{X_i}{L_i} \qquad (10.5)$$

Physical marginal productivities of capital stock are

$$x_{ij} \equiv \frac{\partial X_j}{\partial S_{ij}} = \beta_{ij} \frac{X_j}{S_{ij}} \qquad (10.6)$$

Investment Demand

Let N_j be the present net worth of new capital stock S_{ij} installed by an entrepreneur in the jth industry. Let his desired capital stock be the size of stock maximizing present net worth. First–order conditions for a maximum are

$$n_{ij} \equiv \frac{\partial N_j}{\partial S_{ij}} = 0 \qquad (10.7)$$

Second–order conditions are that the Hessian

$$\begin{vmatrix} \dfrac{\partial n_{1j}}{\partial S_{1j}} & \dfrac{\partial n_{1j}}{\partial S_{2j}} \\[2em] \dfrac{\partial n_{2j}}{\partial S_{1j}} & \dfrac{\partial n_{2j}}{\partial S_{2j}} \end{vmatrix} \qquad (10.8)$$

be positive and its principal minor $\partial n_{1j}/\partial S_{1j}$ negative.

To find desired capital stock proceed as follows. Let entrepreneurs be purely competitive ones, then price P_j of output is beyond their control. At time t, therefore, marginal value productivity of capital stock is $x_{ij}(t)P_j(t)$. As seen from the present time τ marginal value productivity at time t is $x_{ij}(t)P_j(t)e^{-r(t-\tau)}$, where r is the stationary nominal rate of interest used as a discount rate. Define present gross worth of another physical unit of capital stock as the present worth of all future marginal value productivities over its entire useful life:

$$k_{ij}(\tau) \equiv \int_{\tau}^{\infty} x_{ij}(t)P_j(t)e^{-r(t-\tau)} dt \qquad (10.9)$$

Let entrepreneurs expect physical marginal productivity of capital stock to be growing at the stationary rate g_{xij} :

$$x_{ij}\ (t) = x_{ij}\ (\tau)e^{g_{xij}\,(t-\tau)} \tag{10.10}$$

and price of output to be growing at the stationary rate g_{Pj} :

$$P_j(t) = P_j(\tau)e^{g_{Pj}(t-\tau)} \tag{10.11}$$

Insert equations 10.10 and 10.11 into 10.9, define

$$\varrho_{ij}\ \equiv r - (g_{xij}\ + g_{Pj}\ ) \tag{10.12}$$

and write the integral 10.9 as

$$k_{ij}\ (\tau) = \int_\tau^\infty x_{ij}\ (\tau)P_j(\tau)e^{-\varrho_{ij}(t-\tau)}dt$$

Neither $x_{ij}\ (\tau)$ nor $P_j(\tau)$ is a function of t, hence may be taken outside the integral sign. Our g_{xij} , g_{Pj} , and r were all said to be stationary, hence the coefficient ϱ_{ij} of t is stationary, too. Assume $\varrho_{ij}\ > 0$. As a result, find the integral to be

$$k_{ij}\ = x_{ij}\ P_j/\varrho_{ij}$$

Find present net worth of another physical unit of capital stock as its gross worth *minus* its price:

$$n_{ij}\ \equiv k_{ij}\ - P_i\ = x_{ij}\ P_j/\varrho_{ij}\ - P_i \tag{10.13}$$

Appendix 10A proves that equation 10.13 satisfies the second–order conditions for a maximum N_j . Applying the first–order conditions 10.7 to our result 10.13 find equilibrium physical marginal productivity of capital stock

$$x_{ij}\ = \varrho_{ij}\ P_i/P_j \tag{10.14}$$

Take equations 10.14 and 10.6 together and find desired capital stock

$$S_{ij}\ = \beta_{ij}\ P_j X_j/(\varrho_{ij}\ P_i\ ) \tag{10.15}$$

Apply definitions 10.1 and 10.2 to 10.15 and find desired investment as the derivative of desired capital stock with respect to time:

$$I_{ij} \equiv g_{sij} \, S_{ij} = g_{sij} \, \beta_{ij} \, P_j \, X_j / (\varrho_{ij} \, P_i) \qquad (10.16)$$

Equations 10.15 and 10.16 are capital stock and investment desired by an individual entrepreneur in the jth industry. Except X_j everything on the right-hand side of 10.15 and 10.16 is common to all entrepreneurs of the industry. Factor out all common factors, sum over all entrepreneurs of the industry, then X_j becomes industry output, and 10.15 and 10.16 become capital stock and investment desired by the industry.

So investment in the ith good by the industry producing the jth good is in direct proportion to, first, the rate of growth g_{sij} of desired capital stock; second, the elasticity β_{ij} of the output of the jth good with respect to the stock of the ith good; third, the relative price P_j/P_i of the jth and the ith good; and fourth, the output X_j of the jth good. Investment is in inverse proportion to what will turn out to be the real rate of interest ϱ_{ij}.

Consumption Demand

Let every consumer have the utility function

$$U = uC_1^{v_1} C_2^{v_2}$$

where $0 < v_i < 1$, and $u > 0$. Let every consumer spend the fraction c, where $0 < c < 1$, of his money income Y. Then his budget constraint is

$$cY = \sum_{i=1}^{2} (P_i C_i)$$

Maximize the consumer's utility subject to his budget constraint and find his two demand functions

$$C_i = c_i \, Y/P_i \qquad (10.17)$$

where $c_i \equiv cv_i /(v_1 + v_2)$. Equation 10.17 is consumption desired by an individual consumer. Except Y everything on the right-hand side of 10.17 is common to all consumers. Factor out all common factors, sum over all consumers, then Y becomes national money income, and 10.17 becomes national desired consumption. But with immortal capital stock, the entire value of national output represents value added, that is, national money income

$$Y \equiv \sum_{i=1}^{2} (P_i X_i) \qquad (10.18)$$

Insert equation 10.18 into 10.17 and write national desired consumption

$$C_1 = c_1(X_1 + P_2X_2/P_1) \qquad\qquad (10.19)$$

$$C_2 = c_2(P_1X_1/P_2 + X_2) \qquad\qquad (10.20)$$

Goods-Market Equilibrium

Goods-market equilibrium requires output to equal the sum of consumption and investment demand for it:

$$X_i = C_i + \sum_{j=1}^{2} I_{ij} \qquad\qquad (10.21)$$

Employment and the Phillips Function

Let labor employed be the proportion λ of available labor force, where $0 < \lambda < 1$ and λ is so far not a function of time:

$$\sum_{i=1}^{2} L_i = \lambda F \qquad\qquad (10.22)$$

As we saw in chapter 6, a modern Phillips function must have labor's inflationary expectations in it. But unlike chapter 6 this chapter has two goods in it, hence two inflationary expectations g_{Pi}. What should be the weights with which the two expectations should enter the Phillips function? Write equation 10.17 as $c_i = P_i C_i / Y$, where, as we recall $c_i \equiv cv_i /(v_1 + v_2)$, a parameter containing nothing but the propensity to consume c and the exponents v_i of the utility function. In English: c_i are the parametric fractions of income spent on the two goods. Logically we should use those fractions as our weights and write our Phillips function as

$$g_w = p(1 - \lambda)^\pi + c_1 g_{P1} + c_2 g_{P2} \qquad\qquad (10.23)$$

where the coefficient p represents the inflationary potential of the economy and is so far not a function of time, and where $\pi < 0$.

Money

Let the demand for money be a function of national money income and the nominal rate of interest:

$$D = mYr^{\mu} \tag{10.24}$$

where $\mu < 0$, and $m > 0$.

Money–Market Equilibrium

Money-market equilibrium requires the supply of money to equal the demand for it:

$$M = D \tag{10.25}$$

Let us now solve the model for its steady-state equilibrium rates of growth as well as for the levels of its variables at an instant of time.

Steady–State Equilibrium Growth–Rate Solutions

In our derivation of investment demand above, entrepreneurs were using a stationary nominal rate of interest r as a discount rate and expecting price and the physical marginal productivity of capital stock to be growing at stationary rates g_{P_j} and g_{xij}. Are such expectations self-fulfilling? In other words, may the system display steady-state equilibrium growth? It may. By taking derivatives with respect to time of all equations involving the variables C, D, I, x, L, M, P, r, ϱ, S, w, X, and Y the reader may convince himself that the system 10.1 through 10.25 is satisfied by the following steady-state equilibrium growth-rate solutions:

$$g_{Ci} = g_{Xi} \tag{10.26}$$

$$g_D = g_M \tag{10.27}$$

$$g_{Iij} = g_{Xi} \tag{10.28}$$

$$g_{xij} = g_{Xj} - g_{Sij} \tag{10.29}$$

$$g_{Li} = g_F \tag{10.30}$$

$$g_M = g_Y \tag{10.31}$$

$$g_{P1} = g_w - \frac{(1 - \beta_{22})g_{a1} + \beta_{21}g_{a2}}{(1 - \beta_{11})(1 - \beta_{22}) - \beta_{12}\beta_{21}} \tag{10.32}$$

$$g_{P2} = g_w - \frac{(1 - \beta_{11})g_{a2} + \beta_{12}g_{a1}}{(1 - \beta_{11})(1 - \beta_{22}) - \beta_{12}\beta_{21}} \tag{10.33}$$

$$g_r = 0 \tag{10.34}$$

$$g_{\varrho ij} = 0 \tag{10.35}$$

$$g_{Sij} = g_{Xi} \tag{10.36}$$

$$g_w = \frac{p(1 - \lambda)^{\pi}}{1 - c} -$$

$$\frac{[(1 - \beta_{22})c_1 + \beta_{12}c_2]g_{a1} + [(1 - \beta_{11})c_2 + \beta_{21}c_1]g_{a2}}{(1 - c)[(1 - \beta_{11})(1 - \beta_{22}) - \beta_{12}\beta_{21}]} \tag{10.37}$$

$$g_{Xi} = \frac{(1 - \beta_{22})g_{a1} + \beta_{21}g_{a2}}{(1 - \beta_{11})(1 - \beta_{22}) - \beta_{12}\beta_{21}} + g_F \tag{10.38}$$

$$g_{X2} = \frac{(1 - \beta_{11})g_{a2} + \beta_{12}g_{a1}}{(1 - \beta_{11})(1 - \beta_{22}) - \beta_{12}\beta_{21}} + g_F \tag{10.39}$$

$$g_Y = g_F + g_w \tag{10.40}$$

Use our assumptions $0 < c < 1$, $\alpha_1 + \beta_{11} + \beta_{21} = 1$, and $\alpha_2 + \beta_{12} + \beta_{22} = 1$ to show that the denominators of equations 10.32, 10.33, 10.37, 10.38, and 10.39 cannot be zero. Consequently all solutions are meaningful.

Is growth balanced? Use our assumptions $\alpha_1 + \beta_{11} + \beta_{21} = 1$ and $\alpha_2 + \beta_{12} + \beta_{22} = 1$ upon 10.38 and 10.39 to see that

$$g_{X1} \gtrless g_{X2} \quad \text{if } g_{a1}/g_{a2} \gtrless \alpha_1/\alpha_2 \tag{10.41}$$

Growth may be balanced, then, but only by an odd piece of luck. And now let us solve for levels at an instant of time.

Steady-State Equilibrium Growth–Level Solutions

Rates of Interest

Into desired investment 10.16 insert solution 10.36. Then insert desired investment 10.16 and desired consumption 10.19 and 10.20 into the good-market equilibrium condition 10.21, multiply the condition for the first good by P_1 and that for the second by P_2, rearrange and find

$$(1 - c_1 - \beta_{11}g_{X1}/\varrho_{11})P_1X_1 = (c_1 + \beta_{12}g_{X1}/\varrho_{12})P_2X_2 \tag{10.42}$$

$$(c_2 + \beta_{21}g_{X2}/\varrho_{21})P_1X_1 = (1 - c_2 - \beta_{22}g_{X2}/\varrho_{22})P_2X_2 \tag{10.43}$$

Into definition 10.12 insert equation 10.29 and 10.36. Use equations 10.32, 10.33, 10.38, and 10.39 to realize that $g_{P1} + g_{X1} = g_{P2} + g_{X2}$. Use that result to find

$$\varrho_{ij} = r - g_{Pi} \tag{10.44}$$

hence $\varrho_{11} = \varrho_{12} = r - g_{P1}$, and $\varrho_{21} = \varrho_{22} = r - g_{P2}$. So in 10.42 and 10.43 replace ϱ_{12} by ϱ_{11} and ϱ_{21} by ϱ_{22}, respectively. Divide 10.42 by 10.43, getting rid of $P_j X_j$, and find the nonlinear equation

$$\varrho_{11}\varrho_{22} - J_1\varrho_{11} - J_2\varrho_{22} + K = 0 \tag{10.45}$$

where

$$J_1 \equiv [\beta_{22}(1 - c_1) + \beta_{21}c_1]g_{X2}/(1 - c)$$

$$J_2 \equiv [\beta_{11}(1 - c_2) + \beta_{12}c_2]g_{X1}/(1 - c)$$

$$K \equiv (\beta_{11}\beta_{22} - \beta_{12}\beta_{21})g_{X1}g_{X2}/(1 - c)$$

and where, according to equation 10.17, $c \equiv c_1 + c_2$. Use 10.44 to write

$$\varrho_{22} = \varrho_{11} + g_{P1} - g_{P2} \tag{10.46}$$

Insert 10.46 into 10.45 and solve the latter for ϱ_{11} and ϱ_{22}:

$$\varrho_{11} = \frac{J_1 + J_2 - (g_{P1} - g_{P2})}{2}$$

$$\pm \{[\frac{J_1 + J_2 - (g_{P1} - g_{P2})}{2}]^2 + J_2(g_{P1} - g_{P2}) - K\}^{1/2} \tag{10.47}$$

$$\varrho_{22} = \frac{J_1 + J_2 + g_{P1} - g_{P2}}{2}$$

$$\pm \{[\frac{J_1 + J_2 + g_{P1} - g_{P2}}{2}]^2 - J_1(g_{P1} - g_{P2}) - K\}^{1/2} \tag{10.48}$$

where g_{P1} and g_{P2} stand for solutions 10.32 and 10.33. The roots of a quadratic equation may be real or complex and may be positive or nonpositive. In the case of equations 10.47 and 10.48 which will it be? Constraints upon the parameters β_{ij} and c already imposed guarantee that $J_i > 0$ and $K \leq 0$. Consider four possibilities.

First, if $g_{P1} < g_{P2}$ then in equation $10.48 - J_1(g_{P1} - g_{P2}) - K > 0$. Consequently the brace of 10.48 will be positive, and the absolute value of the square root in 10.48 will be greater than $(J_1 + J_2 + g_{P1} - g_{P2})/2$ regardless of the sign of the latter. As a result, 10.48 will have one positive and one negative root, and both will be real.

Second, if $g_{P1} = g_{P2}$ and $K < 0$ the same will be true.

Third, if $g_{P1} = g_{P2}$ and $K = 0$ then equations 10.47 and 10.48 will be identical and will have the positive root $J_1 + J_2$ and the root zero.

Fourth, if $g_{P1} > g_{P2}$ then in equation 10.47 $J_2(g_{P1} - g_{P2}) - K > 0$. Consequently the brace of 10.47 will be positive, and the absolute value of the square root in 10.47 will be greater than $[J_1 + J_2 - (g_{P1} - g_{P2})]/2$ regardless of the sign of the latter. As a result, 10.47 will have one positive and one negative root, and both will be real.

All roots of equations 10.47 and 10.48 are meaningful: we are dividing by 2 and $1 - c$ only, and neither can be zero. Our four possibilities exhaust the universe. Each generates a nonpositive root to be rejected, because it violates the constraint $\varrho_{ij} > 0$ under which the integral 10.9 was taken. But if one side of 10.46 is single-valued, the other must be. Consequently, as constrained, the system has one and only one positive root for every ϱ_{ij}. That root is real and meaningful. Once that root has been found, 10.44 determines the nominal rate of interest r.

Derivation with respect to time of equations 10.44, 10.47, and 10.48 will show that they are stationary, as 10.34 and 10.35 say.

Employment

Write equations 10.42 and 10.43 as

$$\frac{P_1 X_1}{P_2 X_2} = H$$

$$\equiv \frac{c_1 + \beta_{12} g_{X1}/\varrho_{12}}{1 - c_1 - \beta_{11} g_{X1}/\varrho_{11}} = \frac{1 - c_2 - \beta_{22} g_{X2}/\varrho_{22}}{c_2 + \beta_{21} g_{X2}/\varrho_{21}} \tag{10.49}$$

where g_{Xi} stands for 10.38 and 10.39 and ϱ_{ij} for 10.47 and 10.48. Use 10.5 and 10.49 to write $L_1/L_2 = H\alpha_1/\alpha_2$, insert that into 10.22, and find the solutions for employment:

$$L_1 = H\alpha_1\lambda F/(H\alpha_1 + \alpha_2) \tag{10.50}$$

$$L_2 = \alpha_2\lambda F/(H\alpha_1 + \alpha_2) \tag{10.51}$$

Derivation with respect to time of equations 10.50 and 10.51 will show that the latter are indeed growing at the proportionate rate 10.30.

Output

Insert equation 10.49 into desired capital stock 10.15 and find

$$S_{11} = \beta_{11}X_1/\varrho_{11} \tag{10.15a}$$

$$S_{12} = \beta_{12}X_1/(H\varrho_{12}) \tag{10.15b}$$

$$S_{21} = \beta_{21}HX_2/\varrho_{21} \tag{10.15c}$$

$$S_{22} = \beta_{22}X_2/\varrho_{22} \tag{10.15d}$$

which are indeed growing at the proportionate rate 10.36. Insert equations 10.15a through 10.15d into the production functions 10.3 and 10.4 and find the solutions for output

$$X_1 = (G_1^{1-\beta_{22}}G_2^{\beta_{21}})^{1/[(1-\beta_{11})(1-\beta_{22})-\beta_{12}\beta_{21}]} \tag{10.52}$$

$$X_2 = (G_1^{\beta_{12}}G_2^{1-\beta_{11}})^{1/[(1-\beta_{11})(1-\beta_{22})-\beta_{12}\beta_{21}]} \tag{10.53}$$

where

$$G_1 \equiv a_1L_1^{\alpha_1}(\beta_{11}/\varrho_{11})^{\beta_{11}}(\beta_{21}H/\varrho_{21})^{\beta_{21}}$$

$$G_2 \equiv a_2L_2^{\alpha_2}(\beta_{22}/\varrho_{22})^{\beta_{22}}[\beta_{12}/(H\varrho_{12})]^{\beta_{12}}$$

and where H stands for equation 10.49, L_i stands for 10.50 and 10.51, and ϱ_{ij} for 10.47 and 10.48. Derivation with respect to time of 10.52 and 10.53 will show that the latter are indeed growing at the proportionate rates 10.38 and 10.39, respectively.

Relative Prices

Write equation 10.49 as a solution for relative price

$$P_1/P_2 = HX_2/X_1 \tag{10.54}$$

where X_i stands for 10.52 and 10.53. Derivation with respect to time of 10.54 will show that the latter is consistent with 10.32, 10.33, 10.38, and 10.39.

Real Wage Rate

Equation 10.5 will be a solution for the real wage rate w/P_i if L_i stands for 10.50 and 10.51 and X_i for 10.52 and 10.53. Derivation with respect to time of 10.5 will show that the latter is consistent with 10.30, 10.32, 10.33, 10.38, and 10.39.

National Money Income

Write equation 10.5 as $P_i X_i = wL_i /\alpha_i$, insert 10.50 and 10.51, insert result into 10.18, and find national money income

$$Y = w\lambda F(1 + H)/(H\alpha_1 + \alpha_2) \tag{10.55}$$

Derivation with respect to time of 10.55 will show that it is growing at the proportionate rate 10.40.

Required Money Supply

To find the money supply required to uphold steady-state equilibrium growth insert equation 10.24 into 10.25 and find

$$M = mYr^\mu \tag{10.56}$$

where r stands for 10.44 and Y for 10.55. Derivation with respect to time of 10.56 will show that it is growing at the proportionate rate 10.31. Equation 10.56 concludes our solving for growth rates and levels.

Properties of Solutions

Steady-State Growth and Self-fulfilling Expectations

Our growth was steady-state growth, for no right-hand side of our growth-rate solutions 10.26 through 10.40 was a function of time. Our growth implies self-fulfilling expectations. We used the same symbol for the expected and realized values of any variable, implying the equality between the two. Is such equality always possible? Yes, if the system has a set of solutions. No, if the system has no such set. Our system did have the set of solutions 10.26 through 10.56. Specifically our price–wage equilibrium solutions imply two things. First, if entrepreneurs expect labor to adopt the solution value 10.37 of the rate of growth of the money wage rate, then the entrepreneurs will adopt the solution values 10.32 and 10.33 of the rates of growth of prices. Second, if labor expects entrepreneurs to adopt the solution values 10.32 and 10.33, then labor will adopt the solution value 10.37.

Our system has infinitely many solutions, that is, for a given employment fraction λ one for each value of the inflationary potential p, and for a given value of the inflationary potential p one for each employment fraction λ. What difference do λ and p make?

What Difference Does the Employment Fraction λ Make?

At a given inflationary potential p the employment fraction λ makes a difference for certain levels and growth rates.

We begin with levels. According to equations 10.32 and 10.33 g_w and with it λ cancel in the difference $g_{P1} - g_{P2}$ entering our solutions 10.47 and 10.48 for the real rate of interest ϱ_{ij} . Consequently no λ enters into the definition 10.49 of H, and our solutions 10.50 and 10.51 for employment L_i are in direct proportion to λ. Insert those solutions as well as our assumptions $\alpha_1 + \beta_{11} + \beta_{21} = 1$ and $\alpha_2 + \beta_{12} + \beta_{22} = 1$ into our solutions 10.52 and 10.53 for output and find the employment fraction λ entering as a factor raised to the power one. Consequently physical output X_i is in direct proportion to λ. But if employment L_i and physical output X_i are both in direct proportion to λ then in our solutions 10.5 for the real wage rate w/P_i and 10.54 for relative price P_1/P_2 λ will cancel. We just saw that λ canceled in our solutions 10.47 and 10.48 for the real rate of interest ϱ_{ij} . Consequently our solutions 10.15, 10.16, 10.19, and 10.20 for desired physical capital stock S_{ij} , investment I_{ij} , and consumption C_i are in direct proportion to X_i , hence to λ.

Turning to growth rates we find g_w and with it λ to be absent from the growth–rate solutions for the five physical quantities C_i, I_{ij} , L_i, S_{ij}, and X_i. They are also absent from the growth rate $g_w - g_{Pi}$ of the real wage rate w/P_i and from the growth rate $g_{P1} - g_{P2}$ of relative price P_1/P_2: our solutions 10.32 and 10.33 can express those differences in terms containing no λ. But our growth–rate solutions for money supply M, prices P_i , and national money income Y do include g_w and with it λ. Consequently, so does our solution 10.44 for the level of the nominal rate of interest r.

What Difference Does the Inflationary Potential p Make?

At a given employment fraction λ the inflationary potential p makes a difference, too.

Again we begin with levels. According to equations 10.32 and 10.33 g_w and with it p cancel in the difference $g_{P1} - g_{P2}$ entering our solutions 10.47 and 10.48 for the real rate of interest ϱ_{ij}. Consequently p enters into neither the definition 10.49 of H nor solutions 10.50 and 10.51 for employment L_i, solutions 10.52 and 10.53 for output X_i, equations 10.5 for the real wage rate w/P_i, solution 10.54 for relative price P_1/P_2, equations 10.15, 10.16, 10.19, and 10.20 for desired physical capital stock S_{ij}, investment I_{ij}, and consumption C_i.

Turning to growth rates we find g_w and with it p to be absent from the growth rate $g_w - g_{Pi}$ of the real wage rate w/P_i and indeed from all but our growth-rate solutions for money supply M, prices P_i, and national money income Y. Consequently, g_w and with it p are present in our solution 10.44 for the level of the nominal rate of interest r.

Switching from One Steady-State Track to Another

Once settled on any steady-state equilibrium growth track, the economy will tend to stay on it. On such a track, whatever the employment fraction λ is and whatever the inflationary potential p is, expectations are self-fulfilling, and such self-fulfilling expectations are not abandoned easily. They will be abandoned only after new experience has proved them nonself-fulfilling.

Could such new experience be generated by public policy trying to switch the economy from one steady-state equilibrium to another deemed more desirable?

Our answer will be similar to that given in chapter 6. Allowing the employment fraction λ and the inflationary potential p to vary with time, the reader may work out for himself the implications of anti-inflation and employment policies. According to equation 10.15 it remains true that the desired capital coefficients S_{ij}/X_j are in inverse proportion to the real rates of interest ϱ_{ij}. Raising the latter, then, above their equilibrium levels 10.47 and 10.48 will still generate negative excess demand. It remains essentially true that such negative excess demand will not be eliminated by decelerating prices, for if in 10.16, 10.19, and 10.20 P_1 and P_2 were lowered in the same proportion, I_{ij} and C_i would remain unchanged.

Similarly, lowering the real rates of interest ϱ_{ij} below their equilibrium levels 10.47 and 10.48 will generate positive excess demand. It remains essentially true that such positive excess demand will not be eliminated by accelerating physical output, for if in 10.16, 10.19, and 10.20 X_1 and X_2 were raised in the same proportion, I_{ij} and C_i would rise in that proportion.

Once again, the reader will find, anti-inflation policy and employment policy are based on mutually exclusive hopes. Once again the actions taken are mutually exclusive. Once again there is a distinct asymmetry between the two policies. Once the policy interference with equilibrium is terminated and the real rates of interest are restored to their equilibrium levels 10.47 and 10.48, such restoration may undo the original effect of the anti-inflation policy but not that of the employment policy. In this sense the latter is more likely to succeed than the former.

Conclusions

Was the Two-Good Neoclassical Model Meaningful and Operational?

Post–Keynesians notwithstanding, we have built a two-good neoclassical growth model and shown that physical capital stock S_{ij} and its physical marginal productivity x_{ij} remained meaningful as matrices and remained operational in the sense that they helped us find explicit, positive, and real solutions for all our variables.

Our two-good neoclassical model could simulate resource allocation involving substitution among different goods in consumption and production. The model could simulate unbalanced growth, for equation 10.41 showed that growth of physical outputs X_i would be balanced only as an odd piece of luck.

Steady-State Growth in Theory and in National-Income Accounting

Could the model simulate steady-state growth? Clearly yes, as far as the growth of physical outputs X_i is concerned: no right-hand side of our growth-rate solutions 10.38 and 10.39 was a function of time. Clearly yes, as far as the growth of the current value 10.18 of national output is concerned: the right-hand side of our growth-rate solution 10.40 was no function of time either.

But does our model simulate steady-state growth as far as the growth of the value of national output in "constant dollars" is concerned?

How would the U.S. Department of Commerce deflate our Y as defined by equation 10.18? According to the Department of Commerce (1954: 153) "constant dollar series are derived by dividing the current dollar estimates, in as fine a product breakdown as possible, by appropriate price indexes" Let time τ be our base and time t be current time. The Department of Commerce would then divide each term $P_i(t)X_i(t)$ of 10.18 by its own price index $P_i(t)/P_i(\tau)$ and find Y in "constant dollars" to be

$$P_1(\tau)X_1(t) + P_2(\tau)X_2(t) \tag{10.57}$$

Here, for as long as the base time τ is adhered to, $P_i(\tau)$ is stationary. Consequently equation 10.57 will not generally display steady-state growth. A more rapidly growing $X_i(t)$ will eventually swamp a less rapidly growing one, and the growth rate of the sum 10.57 will converge to the growth rate of its most rapidly growing term.

But "eventually" may be a long time—much longer than the period within which the base time τ is adhered to. The Department of Commerce (1973: 3) has used the base years $\tau = 1939$, 1947, 1958, and 1972 and has observed that, just as in our own model, "those output components growing most rapidly tend to show the smallest price increases while those growing least rapidly tend to show the largest price increase. Thus, a recent price base gives greater weight to the slowly growing components than does an earlier price base."

In other words, each time a more recent base year τ is adopted, a more slowly growing term of our equation 10.57 is given a relatively greater weight. The term is so to speak given a new lease of life. A succession of such weight revisions will keep a more rapidly growing $X_i(t)$ from swamping a less rapidly growing one. Indeed, if as an extreme case the base year were changed continuously, then $t = \tau$ and 10.57 would equal 10.18. No deflation would be taking place at all, and we would be back at the steady-state growth of the current value 10.18 of national output! As we have seen earlier, the U.S. gross national product in constant dollars has displayed practically steady-state long-term growth.

Appendix 10A: Second-Order Conditions for a Maximum N_j Are Satisfied

Insert equation 10.6 into 10.13, take the derivatives of n_{ij} defined by 10.13 as ordered by the Hessian 10.8, and write the latter as

$$
\begin{vmatrix}
\beta_{1j}(\beta_{1j} - 1)\dfrac{P_j X_j}{\varrho_{1j}S_{1j}{}^2} & \beta_{1j}\beta_{2j}\dfrac{P_j X_j}{\varrho_{1j}S_{1j}S_{2j}} \\[3ex]
\beta_{1j}\beta_{2j}\dfrac{P_j X_j}{\varrho_{2j}S_{1j}S_{2j}} & \beta_{2j}(\beta_{2j} - 1)\dfrac{P_j X_j}{\varrho_{2j}S_{2j}{}^2}
\end{vmatrix}
$$

$$
= \beta_{1j}\beta_{2j}\dfrac{P_j{}^2 X_j{}^2}{\varrho_{1j}\varrho_{2j}S_{1j}{}^2 S_{2j}{}^2}
\begin{vmatrix}
\beta_{1j} - 1 & \beta_{2j} \\[2ex]
\beta_{1j} & \beta_{2j} - 1
\end{vmatrix}
$$

Use our assumptions $\alpha_j + \beta_{1j} + \beta_{2j} = 1$ to see that the value of the last determinant is α_j. So the Hessian is positive. Since $\beta_{1j} - 1 < 0$, the principal minor of the Hessian is negative.

References

Landesvermessungsamt Schleswig–Holstein, *Topographischer Atlas Schleswig–Holstein,* Neumünster 1963.

U.S. Department of Commerce, *National Income 1954,* Washington, D.C., 1954.

U.S. Department of Commerce, *Long Term Economic Growth 1860–1970,* Washington, D.C., 1973.

H. Uzawa, "On a Two-Sector Model of Economic Growth," I-II, *Rev. Econ. Stud.,* Oct. 1961, *29,* 40–47, and June 1963, *30,* 105–118.

11

Two Countries: International Steady–State but Unbalanced Growth

A professor whose brain is a rarity,
Expounds the exchanges with clarity;
Of his doctrine the flower
Is that Purchasing Power
Is the only true basis of Parity

Anonymous British paper around 1920, Cassel (1940: 265).

The purpose of this chapter is to open the closed economy set out in chapter 6. In one respect international growth is simpler than multisector national growth. In most international trade theory neither labor nor capital is free to move internationally. To Ricardo, such lack of factor mobility was the very rationale for building a separate theory of international trade. To us, such lack of factor mobility is a welcome simplification: we need to worry about the allocation of neither labor nor capital among countries. We do need to worry about the allocation of goods among countries. This problem we shall simplify by assuming the existence of merely two countries, each producing a separate good. A country's good may be invested or consumed. If invested it is not traded internationally but is installed as immortal capital stock in its country of origin. If consumed it may be traded internationally. Each country's consumers consider the two goods good but not perfect substitutes and will consume some of each good. How much will depend upon prices, the exchange rate, and consumer income.

In another respect international growth is more complicated than national growth. The second rationale for a separate theory of international trade was the existence of different monetary units in different countries. This will add another variable to our system, that is, the price of one monetary unit in terms of the other. But it will also add another equation to our system, that is, that a flexible exchange rate will equilibrate the balance of payments.

Much international trade theory is static and lies beyond the scope of this book. Let us at least build a dynamic mini model of international trade admitting three items often ignored even in the few such models that do exist, that is, consumer preferences, disparity of rates of technological progress, and disparity of rates of growth of labor forces. For example, Bardhan (1965) ignored all three items.

Notation

Variables

C_{ij} $\equiv$ physical consumption in jth country of goods produced in ith country

D $\equiv$ demand for money

E $\equiv$ exchange rate in number of monetary units of Country 1 exchanged for one monetary unit of Country 2

g_v $\equiv$ proportionate rate of growth of variable $v \equiv C, D, E, I, \varkappa, L, M, P, r, \varrho, S, w, X,$ and Y

I $\equiv$ physical investment

$\varkappa$ $\equiv$ physical marginal productivity of capital stock

L $\equiv$ labor employed

λ $\equiv$ proportion employed of available labor force

M $\equiv$ supply of money

P $\equiv$ price of goods

p $\equiv$ one coefficent of Phillips function representing inflationary potential

r $\equiv$ nominal rate of interest

ϱ $\equiv$ real rate of interest

S $\equiv$ physical capital stock

U $\equiv$ utility

w $\equiv$ money wage rate

X $\equiv$ physical output

Y $\equiv$ money income

Parameters

a $\equiv$ multiplicative factor of production function

α, β $\equiv$ exponents of production function

c $\equiv$ propensity to consume money income

F $\equiv$ available labor force

g_v $\equiv$ proportionate rate of growth of parameter $v \equiv a$ and F

m $\equiv$ multiplicative factor of demand for money function

μ $\equiv$ exponent of demand for money function

π $\equiv$ exponent of Phillips function

u $\equiv$ multiplicative factor of utility function

υ $\equiv$ exponent of utility function

    Subscripts i and j refer to country number. All parameters are stationary except a and F whose growth rates are stationary.

A Mini Model of International Growth

Definitions

Define the proportionate rate of growth

$$g_v \equiv \frac{dv}{dt} \frac{1}{v} \qquad (11.1)$$

Define investment in the ith country as the derivative of capital stock with respect to time:

$$I_i \equiv \frac{dS_i}{dt} \qquad (11.2)$$

Production

Let entrepreneurs of the ith country apply a Cobb–Douglas production function

$$X_i = a_i L_i{}^{\alpha i} S_i{}^{\beta i} \qquad (11.3)$$

where $0 < \alpha_i < 1; 0 < \beta_i < 1; \alpha_i + \beta_i = 1;$ and $a_i > 0$.

In each country let profit maximization under pure competition equalize real wage rate and physical marginal productivity of labor:

$$\frac{w_i}{P_i} = \frac{\partial X_i}{\partial L_i} = \alpha_i \frac{X_i}{L_i} \qquad (11.4)$$

Physical marginal productivities of capital stock are

$$\varkappa_i \equiv \frac{\partial X_i}{\partial S_i} = \beta_i \frac{X_i}{S_i} \qquad (11.5)$$

Investment Demand

Let N_i be the present worth of new capital stock S_i installed by an entrepreneur in the ith country. Let his desired capital stock be the size of stock maximizing present net worth. Use the stationary nominal rate of interest r_i as a discount rate. Define present gross worth of another physical unit of capital stock as the present worth of all future marginal value productivities of capital stock over its entire useful life. Find present net worth of another physical unit as its gross worth *minus* its price and set it equal to zero, as we did for a closed economy in chapter 6. Desired capital stock will then be

$$S_i = \beta_i X_i / \varrho_i \tag{11.6}$$

where

$$\varrho_i \equiv r_i - (g_{xi} + g_{Pi}) \tag{11.7}$$

Apply definitions 11.1 and 11.2 to equation 11.6 and find desired investment as the derivative of desired capital stock with respect to time:

$$I_i \equiv \frac{dS_i}{dt} = \beta_i g_{xi} X_i / \varrho_i \tag{11.8}$$

Equations 11.6 and 11.8 are capital stock and investment desired by an individual entrepreneur. Except X_i everything on the right–hand side of 11.6 and 11.8 is common to all entrepreneurs of the ith country. Factor out all common factors and sum over all entrepreneurs, then X_i becomes national output, and 11.6 and 11.8 become national desired capital stock and investment.

Consumption Demand

And now for our only international allocation problem, the allocation of consumers' goods between countries. Within each country let all consumers have the same utility function and propensity to consume, but let both differ between countries. In the jth country let every consumer have the utility function

$$U_j = u_j C_{1j}{}^{v_{1j}} C_{2j}{}^{v_{2j}}$$

where $0 < v_{ij} < 1$, and $u_j > 0$. Let every consumer spend the fraction c_j where $0 < c_j < 1$, of his money income Y_j. Then his budget constraint is

$$c_1 Y_1 = P_1 C_{11} + E P_2 C_{21}$$

$$c_2 Y_2 = P_1 C_{12}/E + P_2 C_{22}$$

In the jth country maximize the consumer's utility subject to his budget constraint and find his two demand functions C_{1j} and C_{2j}

$$C_{11} = c_{11} Y_1 / P_1 \qquad\qquad C_{21} = c_{21} Y_1 / (E P_2)$$
$$C_{12} = c_{12} Y_2 / (P_1/E) \qquad\qquad C_{22} = c_{22} Y_2 / P_2$$

where $c_{ij} \equiv c_j v_{ij} /(v_{1j} + v_{2j})$. Here is consumption desired by an individual consumer in the jth country. Except Y_j everything on the right-hand side is common to all consumers of the jth country. Factor out all common factors, sum over all consumers of the jth country, then Y_j becomes national money income of the jth country, and C_{ij} becomes national desired consumption. But with immortal capital stock, the entire value of national output represents value added, that is, national money income

$$Y_j \equiv P_j X_j \qquad (11.9)$$

Insert equation 11.9 and write national desired consumption as the four Graham (1923) demand functions

$$C_{11} = c_{11} X_1 \qquad (11.10)$$

$$C_{12} = c_{12} P_2 X_2 / (P_1/E) \qquad (11.11)$$

$$C_{21} = c_{21} P_1 X_1 / (EP_2) \qquad (11.12)$$

$$C_{22} = c_{22} X_2 \qquad (11.13)$$

Graham demand functions have income and price elasticities of 1 and -1, respectively. Appendix 11A reproduces a few empirical income and price elasticities of demand.

Goods-Market Equilibrium

In each country goods market equilibrium requires the supply of goods to equal the sum of consumption, export, and investment demand for them:

$$X_i = \sum_{j=1}^{2} C_{ij} + I_i \qquad (11.14)$$

Employment and the Phillips Function

In the ith country let labor employed be the proportion λ_i of available labor force, where $0 < \lambda_i < 1$, and λ_i is so far not a function of time:

$$L_i = \lambda_i F_i \qquad (11.15)$$

As we saw in chapter 6, a modern Phillips function must have labor's inflationary expectations in it. But unlike chapter 6 this chapter has two countries and therefore two goods in it. As in chapter 10, two inflationary expectations will be relevant to labor. But unlike chapter 10 this chapter has two different monetary units in it, and the two inflationary expectations are expressed in different monetary units. What matters to labor, however, is the inflationary expectation expressed in labor's domestic monetary unit. That brings the exchange rate right into the Phillips function. What should be the weights with which the two expectations should enter the Phillips function? Recall our $c_{ij} \equiv c_j v_{ij} / (v_{1j} + v_{2j})$, a parameter containing nothing but the propensity to consume c_j and the exponents v_{ij} of the utility function. It follows from our Graham demand functions 11.10 through 11.13 that c_{ij} are the parametric fractions of the income of the jth country spent on the two goods. Logically we should use those fractions as our weights and write our Phillips functions as

$$g_{w1} = p_1(1 - \lambda_1)^{\pi_1} + c_{11}g_{P1} + c_{21}g_{(EP2)} \tag{11.16}$$

$$g_{w2} = p_2(1 - \lambda_2)^{\pi_2} + c_{12}g_{(P1/E)} + c_{22}g_{P2} \tag{11.17}$$

where the coefficients p_i represent inflationary potentials and are so far not functions of time, and where $\pi_i < 0$.

Money

In the ith country let the demand for money be a function of national money income and the nominal rate of interest:

$$D_i = m_i Y_i r_i{}^{\mu i} \tag{11.18}$$

where $\mu_i < 0$, and $m_i > 0$.

Money-market equilibrium requires the supply of money to equal the demand for it:

$$M_i = D_i \tag{11.19}$$

Balance-of-Payments Equilibrium

Balance-of-payments equilibrium requires Country 1's consumption of Country 2's goods to equal Country 2's consumption of Country 1's goods, both being measured in the same monetary unit, or exchange reserves of the ith country would either accumulate or be depleted:

$$EP_2C_{21} = P_1C_{12} \tag{11.20}$$

Let us now solve our model for its steady-state equilibrium rates of growth and interest. Solving it will be facilitated by inserting our Graham demand functions 11.11 and 11.12 into our balance-of-payments equilibrium 11.20 and finding: $E = c_{21}P_1X_1/(c_{12}P_2X_2)$.

Steady-State Equilibrium Growth-Rate and Interest-Rate Solutions

Steady-State Growth

By taking derivatives with respect to time of all equations involving the fourteen variables C_{ij}, D_i, E, I_i, x_i, L_i, M_i, P_i, r_i, ϱ_i, S_i, w_i, X_i, and Y_i the reader may convince himself that the system 11.1 through 11.20 is satisfied by the following growth-rate solutions

$$g_{Cij} = g_{Xi} \tag{11.21}$$

$$g_{Di} = g_{Mi} \tag{11.22}$$

$$g_E = g_{P1} + g_{X1} - (g_{P2} + g_{X2}) \tag{11.23}$$

$$g_{Ii} = g_{Xi} \tag{11.24}$$

$$g_{xi} = 0 \tag{11.25}$$

$$g_{Li} = g_{Fi} \tag{11.26}$$

$$g_{Mi} = g_{Yi} \tag{11.27}$$

$$g_{Pi} = g_{wi} - g_{ai}/\alpha_i \tag{11.28}$$

$$g_{ri} = 0 \tag{11.29}$$

$$g_{\varrho i} = 0 \tag{11.30}$$

$$g_{Si} = g_{Xi} \tag{11.31}$$

$$g_{w1} = \frac{p_1(1 - \lambda_1)^{\pi 1} - c_{11}g_{a1}/\alpha_1 - c_{21}g_{a2}/\alpha_2 + c_{21}(g_{F1} - g_{F2})}{1 - c_1} \tag{11.32}$$

$$g_{w2} = \frac{p_2(1 - \lambda_2)^{\pi 2} - c_{12}g_{a1}/\alpha_1 - c_{22}g_{a2}/\alpha_2 + c_{12}(g_{F2} - g_{F1})}{1 - c_2} \qquad (11.33)$$

$$g_{Xi} = g_{ai}/\alpha_i + g_{Fi} \qquad (11.34)$$

$$g_{Yi} = g_{Fi} + g_{wi} \qquad (11.35)$$

Is growth balanced? In equation 11.34 neither the rates of technological progress g_{ai}, the labor elasticities of output α_i, nor the rates of growth of labor forces g_{Fi} need be the same in the two countries. Growth may be balanced but only as an odd piece of luck.

But it does follow from equations 11.23, 11.28, and 11.34 that when measured in Country 1's monetary unit, the money values of outputs $P_1 X_1$ and $EP_2 X_2$ of the two countries will be growing at the common rate $g_{F1} + g_{w1}$.

Interest Rates

Insert equation 11.25 into 11.7 and find ϱ_i to be nothing but the real rate of interest:

$$\varrho_i = r_i - g_{Pi} \qquad (11.36)$$

Into our goods–market equilibrium 11.14 insert first our balance-of-payments equilibrium 11.20, then our investment demand 11.8 and our Graham demand functions 11.10 through 11.13. Use the definition of v_{ij} to see that $c_{11} + c_{21} \equiv c_1$ and $c_{12} + c_{22} \equiv c_2$. Assume nonzero physical output X_i, divide X_i away, and find the solutions for the real rates of interest

$$\varrho_i = \beta_i g_{Xi}/(1 - c_i) \qquad (11.37)$$

where g_{Xi} stands for our solution 11.34. Insert equation 11.37 into 11.36 and find the solutions for the nominal rates of interest

$$r_i = \beta_i g_{Xi}/(1 - c_i) + g_{Pi} \qquad (11.38)$$

where g_{Pi} stands for our solution 11.28. Insert 11.35 into 11.27 and find the rate of growth of the money supply which would uphold 11.37 and 11.38:

$$g_{Mi} = g_{Fi} + g_{wi} \qquad (11.39)$$

where g_{wi} stands for our solutions 11.32 and 11.33.

Properties of Solutions

Steady-State Growth and Self-fulfilling Expectations

Our growth was steady-state growth, for no right-hand side of our growth-rate solutions 11.21 through 11.35 was a function of time. Our growth implies self-fulfilling expectations. We used the same symbol for the expected and realized values of any variable, implying the equality between the two.

The price-wage equilibrium of a closed economy has now become a price-wage-exchange-rate equilibrium of an open economy. Such a comprehensive equilibrium implies three things. First, if entrepreneurs expect labor to adopt the solution values 11.32 and 11.33 of the rates of growth of the money wage rates, then the entrepreneurs will adopt the solution values 11.28 of the rates of growth of price. Second, if labor expects entrepreneurs to adopt the solution values 11.28 of the rates of growth of price, then labor will adopt the solution values 11.32 and 11.33 of the rates of growth of the money wage rates. Third, the exchange rate will be expected to be growing in accordance with equation 11.23 and will actually be doing so.

Infinitely Many Solutions

Like the systems developed in chapters 6 and 10, our system has infinitely many solutions, that is, for given employment fractions λ_i one for each value of the inflationary potentials p_i, and for given values of the inflationary potentials p_i one for each employment fraction λ_i.

What difference do λ_i and p_i make? We find g_{wi} and with it λ_i and p_i to be absent from the growth-rate solutions for the eight variables C_{ij}, I_i, x_i, L_i, r_i, ϱ_i, S_i, and X_i as well as from solution 11.37 for the level of the real rate of interest.

Is g_{wi} and with it λ_i and p_i also absent from the growth-rate solutions for the real wage rates, of which there are four?

Rates of Growth of Real Wage Rates

In each country there are now two real wage rates, one in terms of the country's own good and one in terms of the imported good.

The ith country's real wage rate in terms of that country's own good is w_i/P_i. Find the growth rate of that real wage rate by writing our solution 11.28 as

$$g_{wi} - g_{Pi} = g_{ai}/\alpha_i \qquad\qquad (11.28)$$

The first country's real wage rate in terms of the second country's good is $w_1/(EP_2)$. Using our solutions 11.23, 11.28, and 11.34 we find the growth rate of that real wage rate to be

$$g_{w1} - (g_E + g_{P2}) = g_{a2}/\alpha_2 + g_{F2} - g_{F1} \qquad\qquad (11.40)$$

The second country's real wage rate in terms of the first country's good is $w_2/(P_1/E)$. Again using our solutions 11.23, 11.28, and 11.34 we find the growth rate of that real wage rate to be

$$g_{w2} - (g_{P1} - g_E) = g_{a1}/\alpha_1 + g_{F1} - g_{F2} \qquad\qquad (11.41)$$

From the growth rates of all four real wage rates, then, g_{wi} and with it λ_i and p_i have disappeared. Each growth rate will be the same for any value of the employment fractions λ_i and inflationary potentials p_i. Friedman's (1968) natural rate of unemployment is not unique in our international economy either.

Let us summarize. Our result 11.28 shows that a country's labor is the better off the more rapidly its own productivity is growing. Our results 11.40 and 11.41 show that a country's labor is the better off the more rapidly productivity and labor force are growing in the other country and the less rapidly the country's own labor force is growing.

Rate of Growth of the Exchange Rate

We find g_{wi} and with it λ_i and p_i to be present in the growth–rate solutions for the remaining six variables, that is, the exchange rate E, money demand D_i and supply M_i, price P_i, money wage rate w_i, and national money income Y_i as well as in our solution 11.38 for the level of the nominal rate of interest.

Of special interest in this chapter is the growth rate of the exchange rate. Find it by inserting equations 11.28 and 11.34 into 11.23:

$$g_E = g_{w1} - g_{w2} + g_{F1} - g_{F2} \qquad\qquad (11.42)$$

The g_{wi} and with it λ_i and p_i of *both* countries is present. A high employment fraction λ_1 or inflationary potential p_1 in the first country will make g_{w1} high and g_E high. A high employment fraction λ_2 or inflationary potential p_2 in the second country will make g_{w2} high and g_E low. Is this the same thing as the purchasing power parity theory?

The Purchasing Power Parity Theory
of the Exchange Rate

The purchasing power parity theory of the exchange rate, formulated by Cassel (1916: 62–65), with a nod of approval by Keynes (footnote, p. 65), said that the rate of growth of the exchange rate would be the rate of growth of price in the first country *minus* the rate of growth of price in the second country.

That is not what our solution 11.23 is saying. We find the rate of growth of the exchange rate to be the sum of the rates of growth of price and physical output in the first country *minus* the sum of the rates of growth of price and physical output in the second country. The purchasing power parity theory left out the rates of growth of physical outputs. Why? Pre-Keynesian theory was more price-conscious than output-conscious. And in all fairness, at the time the purchasing power parity theory was formulated and applied, rates of growth of physical outputs were swamped by rates of growth of prices. Yeager (1958) successfully applied the theory even to the period 1937–1957.

Conclusions

We have internationalized our growth model, but sparingly. Neither labor nor capital moved internationally, and goods moved only in the form of consumers' goods. International demand functions were the simplest possible, that is, of Graham form with income and price elasticities of 1 and -1, respectively. The balance of payments was always in equilibrium, and the equilibrating variable was the exchange rate.

Under such assumptions we found simple solutions for international growth. Growth was always steady-state but was balanced only as an odd piece of luck. The rate of growth of the exchange rate depended on the rates of growth of physical outputs no less than on the rates of growth of prices—a useful supplement to the purchasing power parity theory! Ultimately the rate of growth of the exchange rate was found to depend on the employment fractions λ_i as well as on the inflationary potentials p_i of both countries.

Some major theoretical results of chapter 6 for a closed economy survived the internationalization: each level of the two real—but not of the two nominal—rates of interest ϱ_i was found to be the same for any value of the employment fractions λ_i and the inflationary potentials p_i. So was the rate of growth of each of the four real wage rates w_i/P_i, $w_1/(EP_2)$, and $w_2/(P_1/E)$. As a result, Friedman's natural rate of unemployment was not unique in our international economy either.

Appendix 11A: Empirical Income and Price Elasticities of Demand

Graham demand functions have income and price elasticities of 1 and -1, respectively. Like ourselves, Graham used his demand functions for theoretical convenience and made no attempt at empirical estimation. Empirical elasticities of U.S. import with respect to income were estimated at 0.91 and 1.6 by Ball and Mavwah (1962); at 1.00 by Harberger (1957); at 1.51 by Houthakker and Magee (1969); at 1.27 by Kreinin (1967); and at 1.94, 1.43, and 0.96 by Murray and Ginman (1976).

Elasticities of U.S. import with respect to price were estimated at -0.51 and -1 by Ball and Mavwah (1962); at -0.95 by Harberger (1957); at -0.54 by Houthakker and Magee (1969); at -1.1 by Kreinin (1967); and at -1.23, -0.71, and -1.05 by Murray and Ginman (1976).

Income and price elasticities of the import of fourteen other major countries were estimated at 1.37 and -0.90, respectively, by Houthakker and Magee (1969).

References

R.J. Ball and K. Mavwah, "The U.S. Demand for Imports, 1948–1958," *Rev. Econ. Statist.*, Nov. 1962, *44*, 395–401.

P.K. Bardhan, "Equilibrium Growth in the International Economy," *Quart. J. Econ.*, Aug. 1965, *79*, 455–464.

G. Cassel, "The Present Situation of the Foreign Exchanges," *Econ. J.*, Mar. 1916, *26*, 62–65, with footnote by Keynes, 65.

———, *I förnuftets tjänst*, Stockholm 1940.

M. Friedman, "The Role of Monetary Policy," *Amer. Econ. Rev.*, Mar. 1968, *58*, 1–17.

F.D. Graham, "The Theory of International Values Re-Examined," *Quart. J. Econ.*, Nov. 1923, *38*, 54–86.

A.C. Harberger, "Some Evidence on the International Price Mechanism," *J. Polit. Econ.*, Dec. 1957, *65*, 506–522.

H.S. Houthakker and S.P. Magee, "Income and Price Elasticities in World Trade," *Rev. Econ. Statist.*, May 1969, *51*, 111–125.

M. Kreinin, "Price Elasticities in International Trade," *Rev. Econ. Statist.*, Nov. 1967, *49*, 510–516.

T. Murray and P.J. Ginman, "An Empirical Examination of the Traditional Aggregate Import Demand Model," *Rev. Econ. Statist.*, Feb. 1976, *58*, 75–80.

L.B. Yeager, "A Rehabilitation of Purchasing-Power Parity," *J. Polit., Econ.*, Dec. 1958, *66*, 516–530.

12 Summary and Conclusions

The first four chapters of this book restated four familiar economic models, that is, Wicksell, Keynes, monetarists, and neoclassical growth, of which a synthesis was attempted in chapter 6.

Wicksell: A Dynamic Model of Interest and Inflation

Wicksell's distinction between a natural rate and a money rate of interest enabled him to identify the mechanism through which a quantity theory of money must be operating. A money rate falling short of the natural rate would encourage a demand for money which could be met only by expanding the money supply. Wicksell emphasized this effect by defining a normal rate of interest as the rate which would equalize saving and investment, and presumably require no such expansion of the money supply.

Because Wicksell wanted to deal with inflation, and because inflation is defined as the proportionate rate of growth of price, he needed a dynamic model. He carefully built one by dating his variables and emphasizing the timing of events. Strangely enough, he rejected Fisher's distinction between a nominal rate of interest and a real one. Wicksell considered neither physical output as a variable, liquidity preference, nor cost–push inflation.

Keynes: A Static Model of Interest and Output

Keynes's strength was his variable physical output. Because he did not wish to deal with inflation, he needed neither a dynamic model telling him how rapidly price was changing nor a Fisherian distinction between a nominal rate of interest and a real one.

In Keynes's static equilibrium, interest and physical output were the equilibrating variables. Using a linear form and assuming prices to be frozen, chapter 2 restated such an equilibrium, solved for those variables, and found the familiar sensitivities of the solutions to monetary policy: expanding the money supply would lower the interest rate and raise output.

*Could Keynes and Monetarists Coexist in a
Semidynamic Model of Inflation?*

Borrowing the best from Keynes and the monetarists chapter 3 modified the Keynesian model to accommodate inflation, and with it the two rates of interest. Keynesian-monetarist issues have to do with four variables: the rate of inflation, the two rates of interest, and output. For those four variables algebraic solutions and their sensitivities to monetary policy were found. Expanding the real money supply was found to accelerate inflation, to lower, raise, or leave untouched the nominal rate of interest, to lower the real rate of interest, and to raise output.

Some of the disagreement between Keynesians and monetarists was on parameter values. Keynesians may believe the marginal inducement to invest to be small and the sensitivity of inflation to excess capacity to be low. If such beliefs were correct, expanding the real money supply would lower the nominal rate of interest. Monetarists may believe the opposite, that is, that the marginal inducement to invest is substantial and that the sensitivity of inflation to excess capacity is high; indeed their long-run Phillips curve is virtually vertical. If such beliefs were correct, expanding the real money supply would raise the nominal rate of interest rather than lowering it.

A Fully Dynamic Setting: Neoclassical
Full-Employment Growth

Chapter 3 introduced the absolute minimum of dynamics necessary to accommodate inflation, which was defined as a proportionate rate of growth. But even if not so defined, other variables such as output, capital stock and its marginal productivity, the real wage rate, labor productivity, and the distributive shares deserve to be seen in their natural habitat, a growing economy. For a fully dynamic setting chapter 4 chose the neoclassical growth model, specified it in its crudest possible form, solved it, found its five familiar properties, that is, (1) convergence to steady-state growth of output, (2) identical steady-state growth rates of output and capital stock, (3) stationary rate of return to capital, (4) identical steady-state growth rates of the real wage rate and labor productivity, and (5) stationary distributive shares, and found none of the five properties to be seriously at odds with historical reality.

Neoclassicals and Post-Keynesians: Alternative
Theories of Distribution

Chapter 5 compared the neoclassical full-employment growth model with its closest rival, the post-Keynesian one. The two models were found to have very different sensitivities to the propensity to save. In the neoclassical model, doubling that propensity was found to double the capital coefficient—something on the investment side. In the post-Keynesian model, doubling the propensity was found to halve the profits share—something on the savings side.

The post-Keynesian mark-up factor was found to have a counterpart in the neoclassical model and was merely another variable inherent in the savings-investment adjustment mechanism. An expected Wicksell effect was found in the neoclassical model and a perhaps unexpected one in the post-Keynesian model.

A Kaldorian system was found to impose a heavy burden of adjustment upon the distributive shares, perhaps not actually carried by them. But at least the Kaldorian system was found to be a closed one. By contrast, Joan Robinson's system was found to be an open one, whose very openness appealed to interventionists.

Could Wicksell, Keynes, and Monetarists Coexist in Neoclassical Growth?

Chapter 6—the core of the book—opened the neoclassical growth model to unemployment and inflation and examined the extent to which Wicksellian, Keynesian, monetarist, and neoclassical ideas could coexist in it. In two respects the chapter modified the standard Solow neoclassical growth model set out in chapter 4.

First, the labor market was no longer assumed to clear. Labor employed was the proportion λ of available labor force. A price equation was derived from profit maximization and included the wage expectations of the entrepreneurs. A wage equation was based upon a Phillips function and included the price expectations of labor. A coefficient p of the Phillips function was found to represent the inflationary potential of the economy. Price-wage equilibrium was defined as self-fulfilling expectations.

Second, a bare minimum of monetary arrangements was introduced. There was a money market in which firms might borrow by selling interest-bearing claims upon themselves. Such claims were bought by savers and the monetary authorities alike. The monetary authorities might expand their stock of claims, and with it the money supply, more or less rapidly. The pace at which they expanded it would affect the yield of the claims. The nominal rate of interest was defined as that yield.

Thus modified the neoclassical growth model had an inherent investment function in it. That function was derived and found to be general enough to encompass as special cases Wicksellian, Keynesian, post-Keynesian, and monetarist investment functions.

The system was solved for its rates of growth and interest. The existence and the properties of the solution were examined. Growth was steady-state and implied self-fulfilling expectations. The system had infinitely many solutions, that is, for a given employment fraction λ one for each value of the coefficient p, and for each value of the coefficient p one for each employment fraction λ. But some solutions were unique. Specifically, λ and p were found to be absent from the nine growth-rate solutions for the nominal rate of interest, the real rate of interest, physical consumption, physical investment, physical output, labor employed, physical capital stock, physical marginal productivity of capital stock, and the real wage rate.

Because the real wage rate was growing at the same rate for any value of the employment fraction λ, any value of the unemployment fraction $1 - \lambda$ was a Friedmanian natural rate. Friedman's natural rate was not unique. The employment fraction λ and the inflationary potential p were found to be present in the five growth-rate solutions for the price of goods, the money wage rate, the demand for money, the supply of money, and national money income.

That brought us to the price-wage spiral. Our price-wage equilibrium was represented graphically in figure 6-1 by the intersection between the single price-equation line and one of a family of wage-equation lines. Five possible cases were distinguished. All possible price-wage equilibria were located on the single price-equation line. As a result, with or without inflation labor could have a real wage rate growing at the same rate. In that sense inflation was an empty ritual. Inflation could be depressed to zero by depressing the coefficient p, which was our reason for calling p a measure of the inflationary potential. The value to which p would have to be depressed to eliminate inflation was found to be the higher the higher the rate of technological progress and the lower the employment fraction λ. In other words, high technological progress made inflation fighting easier, but a high employment fraction made it more difficult.

With its infinitely many solutions the system was begging the question of how λ and p were determined. Would they simply be what the monetary authorities allowed them to be? To examine that question the employment fraction λ and the inflationary potential p were at long last allowed to vary with time.

In an effort to reduce the inflationary potential p the monetary authorities would force the money supply to be growing at a rate lower than its steady-state equilibrium value. The hope underlying such an anti-inflation policy was that the price response would dominate the quantity response. In an effort to raise the employment fraction λ the monetary authorities would allow the money supply to be growing at a rate higher than its steady-state equilibrium value. The hope underlying such an employment policy was that the quantity response would dominate the price response.

The dilemma of monetary policy was neatly illustrated by the fact that anti-inflation policy and employment policy were based on mutually exclusive hopes. The actions taken by the monetary authorities under the two policies were mutually exclusive: one policy was the other in reverse. But between the effects of the two policies there was a distinct asymmetry: actual physical capital stock was able to adjust to desired physical capital stock under negative excess demand but unable to do so under positive excess demand. As a result, once the policy interference with equilibrium was terminated and the real rate of interest was restored to its equilibrium level, such restoration might undo the original effect of an anti-inflation policy but not that of an employment policy. In this sense the latter was more likely to succeed than the former.

The model set out in chapter 6 was Wicksellian, but only in the sense that it determined an interest rate at which saving equaled investment. That equality guaranteed neither full employment nor absence of inflation.

Was the model Keynesian? Yes, in the sense that output was bounded by demand and touched no supply bound. Was demand controllable? Certainly! The monetary authorities could generate negative and positive excess demand. But they could not control the response to such excess demand.

Was the model monetarist? Yes, in the sense that it could generate inflation and that it distinguished between a nominal and a real rate of interest. But Friedman's natural rate of unemployment was not unique. And the asymmetry between the anti-inflation policy and the employment policy was the result of an Austrian capital theory inherent in a neoclassical growth model but absent from Keynesian and monetarist models alike.

Was the model neoclassical? Yes, in the sense that it simulated labor-capital substitution in a steady-state equilibrium growth setting and had an Austrian capital theory built into it according to which the desired capital coefficient was in inverse proportion to the real rate of interest. But in one respect our model was not neoclassical: it had room for involuntary unemployment. It had infinitely many solutions, offering scope for controlling demand.

*A Corporate Economy: Inflation,
Bonds, and Shares*

In chapters 4 through 6 all saving was presumably personal saving, and its placement was presumably interest-bearing. Chapter 7 introduced corporate finance in a steady-state growth and inflation model.

According to Fisher the present worth of a financial asset would depend solely on the sum of the discounted future cash flows paid to its owner. Fisher's principle was used to find the price of a bond as capitalized interest, to find the price of a share as capitalized dividends, and to find the

dollar proceeds of new bond and share issues. Assuming stationary fractions of investment to be financed by bond and share issues, chapter 7 then
determined the fractions, also stationary, of profits absorbed by the interest
and dividend bills. The algebraic relationship between the two pairs of fractions turned out to be very sensitive to the rate of inflation and revealed a
fundamental difference between bond and share financing. If, under inflation, a corporation financed the fraction H_b of its investment by issuing
bonds, the interest on them was found to absorb annually a fraction of
profits less than H_b . But if the corporation financed the fraction H_s of its
investment by issuing shares, the dividends on them were found to absorb
annually a fraction of profits equal to H_s . Thus inflation would tilt the
debt-equity ratio in favor of debt—the more so the higher the rate of
steady-state inflation. The finding was nontrivial: it included an assumption that the nominal rate of interest was always fully adjusted to a perfectly
foreseen rate of steady-state inflation.

One by-product of the assumptions underlying chapter 7 was the testable proposition, tested in appendix 7A, that the bond and dividend yields
were practical representatives of the nominal and real rates of interest,
respectively. Another by-product was the testable proposition, tested in
appendix 7B, that share prices and goods prices were growing at the same
rate.

Mortal Capital Stock: Gross and Net Investment

Chapter 1 confined itself to point-input point-output capital stock. Chapters 2 and 3 mentioned investment but never capital stock. Chapters 4
through 7 assumed capital stock to be immortal. Under steady-state growth
chapter 8 examined what difference it would make to growth rates, investment, and interest rates if capital stock were mortal. By and large, the theoretical results of chapter 6 would still stand, although the mathematics
expressing them became a bit more involved. Perhaps that would be a price
worth paying for moving one step closer to gross national accounting data,
usually considered more accurate than net ones.

Nature and Growth: Exhaustible and Nonexhaustible Natural Resources

Chapters 1 through 8 ignored nature. Chapters 4 through 8 found steady-
state growth to be possible. But such growth is explosive. By contrast, a
nonexhaustible natural resource like land is stationary, and an exhaustible
one like fossil fuels is being absorbed in the production process. Must some-

thing growing without bounds eventually swamp anything stationary or even dwindling?

Growth optimism based on geological and technological potential merely asserts that what is finite is very large indeed. Neither geology nor technology alone can remove the logical conflict between finite resources and growth without bounds. Only economics can do that, and chapter 9 tried to do it.

Assuming, first, growing technology; second, growing labor force; third, steady-state dwindling extraction of minerals making useful life of mines rise without bounds; and fourth, that man-made and natural resources are good albeit not perfect substitutes; we demonstrated that steady-state growth of physical output and the real wage rate was both feasible and profitable.

Dwindling natural resources could be one of the causes of inflation: our solution for the rate of inflation was found to be the higher the more rapidly natural resources were dwindling.

Contrary to popular beliefs, immiserization would be a remote possibility in advanced economies but perhaps a distinct one in backward preindustrial economies.

Two Goods: Steady-State
but Unbalanced Growth

According to post-Keynesians, one-good neoclassical growth models such as those used in chapters 4 through 9 would break down as soon as the number of goods contained in them was raised beyond one. Aggregate physical capital stock and its physical marginal productivity could then no longer be expressed as meaningful and operational single numbers.

To demonstrate that such single numbers are unnecessary, chapter 10 built a two-good neoclassical growth model in which physical capital stock and its physical marginal productivity remained meaningful as matrices and remained operational in the sense that they helped find explicit, positive, and real solutions for all variables of the model.

The two-good neoclassical model of chapter 10 could simulate resource allocation involving substitution among different goods in consumption and production, and it could simulate steady-state but unbalanced growth.

Two Countries: International Steady-State
but Unbalanced Growth

Chapters 1 through 10 assumed the economy to be a closed one. Chapter 11 introduced the bare minimum of an international economy. It assumed the existence of merely two countries, each producing a separate good. If consumed the good was traded internationally. Each country's consumers considered the two goods good but not perfect substitutes and would consume some of each. How much would depend upon prices, the exchange rate, and consumer income. A flexible exchange rate would equilibrate the balance of payments.

Solutions were found for the rates of growth and interest. International growth would be steady–state but would be balanced only as an odd piece of luck. The rate of growth of each of the four real wage rates was found to be the same for any value of the employment fractions λ_i and the inflationary potentials p_i. As a result, again Friedman's natural rate of unemployment was not unique.

The rate of growth of the exchange rate was found to depend upon the rates of growth of physical outputs no less than upon the rates of growth of prices. Ultimately the rate of growth of the exchange rate was found to depend upon the employment fractions λ_i and the inflationary potentials p_i of both countries.

Index

About the Author

Hans Brems was born in Denmark and has been a U.S. citizen since 1958. He received the Ph.D. from the University of Copenhagen and taught at the University of California, Berkeley, from 1951 to 1954, when he came to the University of Illinois. During the sixties and seventies he was a visiting professor at the University of Colorado and Harvard; and abroad at the Universities of Copenhagen, Denmark; Göttingen, Hamburg, and Kiel, in Germany; and Göteborg, Lund, and Uppsala, in Sweden. In the spring of 1980 he will be a visiting professor at the Stockholm School of Economics.

Dr. Brems has written several articles for the following journals: *American Economic Review, Econometrica, Economic Journal, Quarterly Journal of Economics,* and *Review of Economics and Statistics,* and has written numerous articles for other professional journals at home and abroad. He wrote the article "Economics" in the *Encyclopedia Americana.* His books include: *Product Equilibrium under Monopolistic Competition* (Harvard 1951); *Output, Employment, Capital, and Growth* (Harper 1959, Greenwood 1973); *Quantitative Economic Theory* (Wiley 1968); *Økonomiske langtidsperspektiver* (Sparevirke, Copenhagen 1971); *Labor, Capital, and Growth* (Lexington Books, Heath 1973); and *A Wage Earners' Investment Fund: Forms and Economic Effects* (Sveriges Industriförbund, Stockholm 1975).